Promises for
Peace Officers

Promises for Peace Officers

From the Old and New Testaments of The New King James Version of the Holy Bible

Scripture taken from the New King James Version®, Copyright ©1982 by Thomas Nelson, Inc. Used by permission. All rights reserved.

Copyright © 2015 Judy La Salle

ISBN – 13: 9781500987763
ISBN – 10: 150098776X
Library of Congress Control Number: 2015907331
CreateSpace Independent Publishing Platform
North Charleston, South Carolina

All Scripture is given by inspiration of God, and is profitable for doctrine, for reproof, for correction, for instruction in righteousness, that the man of God may be complete, thoroughly equipped for every good work.

2 Timothy 3:16-17

Table of Contents

WHAT THE BIBLE SAYS ABOUT . . . 1
Salvation · · · · · · · · · · · · · · · · · 2
Breaking the Law · · · · · · · · · · · 5
Various Crimes · · · · · · · · · · · · 10
The Appropriateness of
Punishment · · · · · · · · · · · · · · · 41
The Officer's Authority · · · · · · · 47
Being Armed · · · · · · · · · · · · · · 52
Your Conduct as an Officer · · · · · 58

WHEN YOU ARE CALLED TO . . . 63
Interact with the Public · · · · · · · 64

Respond to Domestic
Disturbances · · · · · · · · · · · · · · · · 69
Deal With Victims, Injury
and Death · · · · · · · · · · · · · · · · · · · 75
Use Informants/
Work Undercover · · · · · · · · · · · · 82
Make an Arrest · · · · · · · · · · · · · · 88
Control Prisoners · · · · · · · · · · · · 95
Handle Evidence/Contraband · · · 99
Investigate · · · · · · · · · · · · · · · · · 103
Write Reports · · · · · · · · · · · · · · 108
Testify in Court · · · · · · · · · · · · · 112
Conduct an Internal Affairs
Investigation/Administer
Discipline · · · · · · · · · · · · · · · · · ·117
Deal with Superiors · · · · · · · · · · 123
Deal with Subordinates · · · · · · · 129
Share Your Faith · · · · · · · · · · · · 135

WHEN YOU ARE . . . · · · · · · · · · · · · · 141
Reviled and Persecuted · · · · · · · 142

Angry	151
Discouraged	156
Under Stress	163
Burned Out	169
Hardened/Embittered	175
Impressed with Your Own Authority	181
The Subject of an Internal Affairs Investigation	187

WHEN YOU NEED ... 195

Protection	196
Courage	201
Strength	207
Wisdom	212
Self-Control	218
Faith	223
Forgiveness	229
Joy	234

What The Bible Says About . . .

What The Bible Says About . . .
SALVATION

But as many as received Him, to them He gave the right to become children of God, to those who believe in His name:

John 1:12

Jesus answered and said to him, "Most assuredly, I say to you, unless one is born again, he cannot see the kingdom of God."

John 3:3

For God so loved the world that He gave His only begotten Son, that whoever believes in Him should not perish but have everlasting life.

John 3:16

Most assuredly, I say to you, he who believes in Me has everlasting life.
John 6:47

Jesus said to him, "Thomas, because you have seen Me, you have believed. Blessed are those who have not seen and yet have believed."
John 20:29

Therefore, if anyone is in Christ, he is a new creation; old things have passed away; behold, all things have become new.
2 Corinthians 5:17

And you, being dead in your trespasses and the uncircumcision of your flesh, He has made alive together with Him, having forgiven you all trespasses,
Colossians 2:13

But God, who is rich in mercy, because of His great love with which He loved us, even when we were dead in trespasses, made us alive together with Christ (by grace you have been saved),
Ephesians 2:4-5

But if we walk in the light as He is in the light, we have fellowship with one another, and the blood of Jesus Christ His Son cleanses us from all sin.
1 John 1:7

In this is love, not that we loved God, but that He loved us and sent His Son to be the propitiation for our sins.
1 John 4:10

What The Bible Says About . . .
BREAKING THE LAW

Whoever will not observe the law of your God and the law of the king, let judgment be executed speedily on him, whether it be death, or banishment, or confiscation of goods, or imprisonment.
Ezra 7:26

These six things the Lord hates, Yes, seven are an abomination to Him: A proud look, A lying tongue, Hands that shed innocent blood, A heart that devises wicked plans, Feet that are swift in running to evil, A false witness who speaks lies, And one who sows discord among brethren.
Proverbs 6:16-19

People do not despise a thief If he steals to satisfy himself when he is starving. Yet when he is found, he must restore sevenfold; He may have to give up all the substance of his house.

Proverbs 6:30-31

To do evil is like sport to a fool, But a man of understanding has wisdom.

Proverbs 10:23

Because the sentence against an evil work is not executed speedily, therefore the heart of the sons of men is fully set in them to do evil.

Ecclesiastes 8:11

Agree with your adversary quickly, while you are on the way with him, lest your

adversary deliver you to the judge, the judge hand you over to the officer, and you be thrown into prison. Assuredly, I say to you, you will by no means get out of there till you have paid the last penny.
Matthew 5:25-26

For since the creation of the world His invisible attributes are clearly seen, being understood by the things that are made, even His eternal power and Godhead, so that they are without excuse,
Romans 1:20

being filled with all unrighteousness, sexual immorality, wickedness, covetousness, maliciousness; full of envy, murder, strife, deceit, evil-mindedness; they are whisperers, backbiters, haters of God, violent, proud, boasters, inventors of evil things, disobedient to parents, undiscerning, untrustworthy, unloving, unforgiving, unmerciful; who, knowing the righteous judgment of God, that those who practice such things are deserving of death, not only do the same but also approve of those who practice them.

Romans 1:29-32

Therefore whoever resists the authority resists the ordinance of God, and those who resist will bring judgment on themselves.

Romans 13:2

knowing this: that the law is not made for a righteous person, but for the lawless and insubordinate, for the ungodly and

for sinners, for the unholy and profane, for murderers of fathers and murderers of mothers, for manslayers, for fornicators, for sodomites, for kidnappers, for liars, for perjurers, and if there is any other thing that is contrary to sound doctrine,
1 Timothy 1:9-10

What The Bible Says About . . .
VARIOUS CRIMES

Murder

Whoever sheds man's blood, By man his blood shall be shed; For in the image of God He made man.

Genesis 9:6

Thou shalt not kill.

Exodus 20:13 (KJV)

But if anyone hates his neighbor, lies in wait for him, rises against him and strikes him mortally, so that he dies, and he flees to one of these cities, then the elders of his city shall send and bring him from there, and deliver him over to the hand of the avenger of blood, that he may die.

Deuteronomy 19:11-12

How much more, when wicked men have killed a righteous person in his own house on his bed? Therefore, shall I not now require his blood at your hand and remove you from the earth?

2 Samuel 4:11

The murderer rises with the light; He kills the poor and needy; And in the night he is like a thief.

Job 24:14

But let none of you suffer as a murderer, a thief, an evildoer, or as a busybody in other people's matters.

1 Peter 4:15

Whoever hates his brother is a murderer, and you know that no murderer has eternal life abiding in him.

1 John 3:15

Manslaughter

He who strikes a man so that he dies shall surely be put to death. However, if he did not lie in wait, but God delivered him into his hand, then I will appoint for you a place where he may flee. But if a man acts with premeditation against his neighbor, to kill him by treachery, you shall take him from My altar, that he may die.

Exodus 21:12-14

then you shall appoint cities to be cities of refuge for you, that the manslayer who kills any person accidentally may flee there. They shall be cities of refuge for you from the avenger, that the manslayer may not die until he stands before the congregation in judgment.

Numbers 35:11-12

These six cities shall be for refuge for the children of Israel, for the stranger, and for the sojourner among them, that anyone who kills a person accidentally may flee there . . . However, if he pushes him suddenly without enmity, or throws anything at him without lying in wait, or uses a stone, by which a man could die, throwing it at him without seeing him, so that he dies, while he was not his enemy or seeking his harm, then the congregation shall judge between the manslayer and the avenger of blood according to these judgments. So the congregation shall deliver the manslayer from the hand of the avenger of blood, and the congregation shall return him to the city of refuge where he had fled, and he shall remain there until the death of the high priest who was anointed with the holy oil.

Numbers 35:15, 22-25

And this is the case of the manslayer who flees there, that he may live: Whoever kills his neighbor unintentionally, not having hated him in time past– as when a man goes to the woods with his neighbor to cut timber, and his hand swings a stroke with the ax to cut down the tree, and the head slips from the handle and strikes his neighbor so that he dies–he shall flee to one of these cities and live; lest the avenger of blood, while his anger is hot, pursue the manslayer and overtake him, because the way is long, and kill him, though he was not deserving of death, since he had not hated the victim in time past.

Deuteronomy 19:4-6

Assault and Battery/Violence/ Arson

Cursed is the one who attacks his neighbor secretly

Deuteronomy 27:24a

If men contend with each other, and one strikes the other with a stone or with his fist, and he does not die but is confined to his bed, if he rises again and walks about outside with his staff, then he who struck him shall be acquitted. He shall only pay for the loss of his time, and shall provide for him to be thoroughly healed.

Exodus 21:18-19

If men fight, and hurt a woman with child, so that she gives birth prematurely, yet no harm follows, he shall surely be punished accordingly as the woman's husband imposes on him; and he shall pay as the judges determine. But if any harm follows, then you shall give life for life,

Exodus 21:22-23

If fire breaks out and catches in thorns, so that stacked grain, standing grain, or the field is consumed, he who kindled the fire shall surely make restitution.

Exodus 22:6

The Lord tests the righteous, But the wicked and the one who loves violence His soul hates.

Psalm 11:5

They have set fire to Your sanctuary; They have defiled the dwelling place of Your name to the ground. They said in their hearts, "Let us destroy them altogether." They have burned up all the meeting places of God in the land . . . Remember this, that the enemy has reproached, O Lord, And that a foolish people has blasphemed Your name.

Psalm 74:7-8, 18

Thus says the Lord: "Execute judgment and righteousness, and deliver the plundered out of the hand of the oppressor. Do no wrong and do no violence to the stranger, the fatherless, or the widow, nor shed innocent blood in this place.
Jeremiah 22:3

Thus says the Lord God: "Enough, O princes of Israel! Remove violence and plundering, execute justice and righteousness, and stop dispossessing My people," says the Lord God.
Ezekiel 45:9

Theft/Extortion/ Embezzlement

Thou shalt not steal.
> *Exodus 20:15 (KJV)*

If a man delivers to his neighbor money or articles to keep, and it is stolen out of the man's house, if the thief is found, he shall pay double. If the thief is not found, then the master of the house shall be brought to the judges to see whether he has put his hand into his neighbor's goods.
> *Exodus 22:7-8*

And the Lord spoke to Moses, saying: "If a person sins and commits a trespass against the Lord by lying to his neighbor about what was delivered to him for safekeeping, or about a pledge, or about a robbery, or if he has extorted from his neighbor, or if he has found what was lost and lies concerning it, and swears falsely–in any one of these things that a man may do in which he sins: then it shall be, because he has sinned and is guilty, that he shall restore what he has stolen, or the thing which he has extorted, or what was delivered to him for safekeeping, or the lost thing which he found, or all that about which he has sworn falsely. He shall restore its full value, add one-fifth more to it, and give it to whomever it belongs, on the day of his trespass offering.

Leviticus 6:1-5

Whoever is a partner with a thief hates his own life; He swears to tell the truth, but reveals nothing.

Proverbs 29:24

In you they take bribes to shed blood; you take usury and increase; you have made profit from your neighbors by extortion, and have forgotten Me, says the Lord God.

Ezekiel 22:12

Woe to you, scribes and Pharisees, hypocrites! For you cleanse the outside of the cup and dish, but inside they are full of extortion and self-indulgence.

Matthew 23:25

Let him who stole steal no longer, but rather let him labor, working with his hands what is good, that he may have something to give him who has need.

Ephesians 4:28

Substance Abuse

Harlotry, wine, and new wine enslave the heart.

Hosea 4:11

Wine is a mocker, Strong drink is a brawler, And whoever is led astray by it is not wise.

Proverbs 20:1

Who has woe? Who has sorrow? Who has contentions? Who has complaints? Who has wounds without cause? Who has redness of eyes? Those who linger long at the wine, Those who go in search of mixed wine . . . At the last it bites like a serpent, And stings like a viper. Your eyes will see strange things, And your heart will utter perverse things.

Yes, you will be like one who lies down in the midst of the sea, Or like one who lies at the top of the mast, saying: "They have struck me, but I was not hurt; They have beaten me, but I did not feel it. When shall I awake, that I may seek another drink?"

Proverbs 23:29-30, 32-36

Give strong drink unto him that is ready to perish, and wine unto those that be of heavy hearts.

Proverbs 31:6 (KJV)

Woe to those who rise early in the morning, That they may follow intoxicating drink; Who continue until night, till wine inflames them!

Isaiah 5:11

But they also have erred through wine, And through intoxicating drink are out of the way; The priest and the prophet have erred through intoxicating drink, They are swallowed up by wine, They are out of the way through intoxicating drink; They err in vision, they stumble in judgment. For all tables are full of vomit and filth; No place is clean.

Isaiah 28:7-8

I beseech you therefore, brethren, by the mercies of God, that you present your bodies a living sacrifice, holy, acceptable to God, which is your reasonable service.

Romans 12:1

Lying/Perjury

You shall not bear false witness against your neighbor.
Exodus 20:16

And you shall not swear by My name falsely, nor shall you profane the name of your God: I am the Lord.
Leviticus 19:12

So the king said to him, "How many times shall I make you swear that you tell me nothing but the truth in the name of the Lord?"
1 Kings 22:16

I hate and abhor lying, But I love Your law.
Psalm 119:163

Therefore, putting away lying, "Let each one of you speak truth with his neighbor," for we are members of one another.
Ephesians 4:25

Sex Offenses/Incest/Prostitution/ Bestiality/Rape

None of you shall approach anyone who is near of kin to him, to uncover his nakedness: I am the Lord.
Leviticus 18:6

Do not prostitute your daughter, to cause her to be a harlot, lest the land fall into harlotry, and the land become full of wickedness.
Leviticus 19:29

If a man mates with an animal, he shall surely be put to death, and you shall kill the animal. If a woman approaches any animal and mates with it, you shall kill the woman and the animal. They shall surely be put to death. Their blood is upon them.
Leviticus 20:15-16

As they were enjoying themselves, suddenly certain men of the city, perverted men, surrounded the house and beat on the door. They spoke to the master of the house, the old man, saying, "Bring out the man who came to your house, that we may know him carnally!" But the man, the master of the house, went out to them and said to them, "No, my brethren! I beg you, do not act so wickedly! Seeing this man has come into my house, do not commit this outrage. Look, here is my virgin daughter and the man's concubine; let me bring them out now. Humble them, and do with them as you please; but to this man do not do such a vile thing!" But the men would not heed him. So the man took his concubine and brought her out to them. And they knew her and abused her all night until morning; and when the day began to break, they let her go. Then the woman came as the day was dawning, and fell down at the door of the man's house where her master was, till it was light . . . And so it was that all who saw it said, "No such deed has been done or seen from the day that the children of Israel came up from the land of Egypt until this day. Consider it, confer, and speak up!"

Judges 19:22-26, 30

Flee sexual immorality. Every sin that a man does is outside the body, but he who commits sexual immorality sins against his own body.

1 Corinthians 6:18

For men will be lovers of themselves, lovers of money, boasters, proud, blasphemers, disobedient to parents, unthankful, unholy, unloving, unforgiving, slanderers, without self-control, brutal, despisers of good, traitors, headstrong, haughty, lovers of pleasure rather than lovers of God, having a form of godliness but denying its power. And from such people turn away! For of this sort are those who creep into households and make captives of gullible women loaded down with sins, led away by various lusts,

2 Timothy 3:2-6

And saw among the simple, I perceived among the youths, A young man devoid of understanding . . . And there a woman met him, With the attire of a harlot, and a crafty heart . . . Immediately he went after her, as an ox goes to the slaughter, Or as a fool to the correction of the stocks, Till an arrow struck his liver. As a bird hastens to the snare, He did not know it would cost his life . . . Her house is the way to hell, Descending to the chambers of death.

Proverbs 7:7, 10, 22-23, 27

Marriage is honorable among all, and the bed undefiled; but fornicators and adulterers God will judge.

Hebrews 13:4

Graft/Corruption

You shall not cheat your neighbor, nor rob him. The wages of him who is hired shall not remain with you all night until morning . . . You shall do no injustice in judgment. You shall not be partial to the poor, nor honor the person of the mighty. In righteousness you shall judge your neighbor. You shall not go about as a talebearer among your people; nor shall you take a stand against the life of your neighbor: I am the Lord.

Leviticus 19:13, 15-16

Now it came to pass when Samuel was old that he made his sons judges over Israel . . . But his sons did not walk in his ways; they turned aside after dishonest gain, took bribes, and perverted justice.

1 Samuel 8:1, 3

In you they take bribes to shed blood; you take usury and increase; you have made profit from your neighbors by extortion, and have forgotten Me, says the Lord God.

Ezekiel 22:12

Indeed the wages of the laborers who mowed your fields, which you kept back by fraud, cry out; and the cries of the reapers have reached the ears of the Lord of Sabaoth.

James 5:4

Cruelty to Animals

Then the man came to the house. And he unloaded the camels, and provided straw and feed for the camels . . .
Genesis 24:32a

You shall not muzzle an ox while it treads out the grain.
Deuteronomy 25:4

A righteous man regards the life of his animal, But the tender mercies of the wicked are cruel.
Proverbs 12:10

Then He said to them, "What man is there among you who has one sheep, and if it falls into a pit on the Sabbath, will not lay hold of it and lift it out?

Matthew 12:11

So He spoke this parable to them, saying: "What man of you, having a hundred sheep, if he loses one of them, does not leave the ninety-nine in the wilderness, and go after the one which is lost until he finds it? And when he has found it, he lays it on his shoulders, rejoicing. And when he comes home, he calls together his friends and neighbors, saying to them, 'Rejoice with me, for I have found my sheep which was lost!'

Luke 15:3-6

Juvenile Offenses/Beyond Control

Honor your father and your mother, that your days may be long upon the land which the Lord your God is giving you.
Exodus 20:12

If a man has a stubborn and rebellious son who will not obey the voice of his father or the voice of his mother, and who, when they have chastened him, will not heed them, then his father and his mother shall take hold of him and bring him out to the elders of his city, to the gate of his city. And they shall say to the elders of his city, 'This son of ours is stubborn and rebellious; he will not obey our voice; he is a glutton and a drunkard.'
Deuteronomy 21:18-20

For I have told him that I will judge his house forever for the iniquity which he knows, because his sons made themselves vile, and he did not restrain them.

1 Samuel 3:13

The Proverbs of Solomon: A wise son makes a glad father, But a foolish son is the grief of his mother.

Proverbs 10:1

A wise son heeds his father's instruction, But a scoffer does not listen to rebuke.

Proverbs 13:1

Chasten your son while there is hope, And do not set your heart on his destruction.

Proverbs 19:18

He who mistreats his father and chases away his mother Is a son who causes shame and brings reproach.

Proverbs 19:26

Even a child is known by his deeds, Whether what he does is pure and right.

Proverbs 20:11

Train up a child in the way he should go, And when he is old he will not depart from it.

Proverbs 22:6

The eye that mocks his father, And scorns obedience to his mother, The ravens of the valley will pick it out, And the young eagles will eat it.

Proverbs 30:17

And not many days after, the younger son gathered all together, journeyed to a far country, and there wasted his possessions with prodigal living. But when he had spent all, there arose a severe famine in that land, and he began to be in want. Then he went and joined himself to a citizen of that country, and he sent him into his fields to feed swine. And he would gladly have filled his stomach with the pods that the swine ate, and no one gave him anything. But when he came to himself, he said, 'How many of my father's hired servants have bread enough and to spare, and I perish with hunger! I will arise and go to my father, and will say to him, "Father, I have sinned against heaven and before you, and I am no longer worthy to be called your son. Make me like one of your hired servants."'

And he arose and came to his father. But when he was still a great way off, his father saw him and had compassion, and ran and fell on his neck and kissed him.
Luke 15:13-20

being filled with all unrighteousness, sexual immorality, wickedness, covetousness, maliciousness; full of envy, murder, strife, deceit, evil-mindedness; they are whisperers, backbiters, haters of God, violent, proud, boasters, inventors of evil things, disobedient to parents, undiscerning, untrustworthy, unloving, unforgiving, unmerciful; who, knowing the righteous judgment of God, that those who practice such things are deserving of death, not only do the same but also approve of those who practice them.
Romans 1:29-32

Children, obey your parents in the Lord, for this is right.

Ephesians 6:1

And you, fathers, do not provoke your children to wrath, but bring them up in the training and admonition of the Lord.

Ephesians 6:4

Fathers, do not provoke your children, lest they become discouraged.

Colossians 3:21

What The Bible Says About . . .
THE APPROPRIATENESS OF PUNISHMENT

Whoever is deserving of death shall be put to death on the testimony of two or three witnesses; he shall not be put to death on the testimony of one witness.
Deuteronomy 17:6

According to the sentence of the law in which they instruct you, according to the judgment which they tell you, you shall do; you shall not turn aside to the right hand or to the left from the sentence which they pronounce upon you.
Deuteronomy 17:11

Fathers shall not be put to death for their children, nor shall the children be put to death for their fathers; a person shall be put to death for his own sin.

Deuteronomy 24:16

If there is a dispute between men, and they come to court, that the judges may judge them, and they justify the righteous and condemn the wicked,

Deuteronomy 25:1

People do not despise a thief If he steals to satisfy himself when he is starving. Yet when he is found, he must restore sevenfold; He may have to give up all the substance of his house.

Proverbs 6:30-31

In mercy and truth Atonement is provided for iniquity; And by the fear of the Lord one departs from evil.

Proverbs 16:6

Because the sentence against an evil work is not executed speedily, therefore the heart of the sons of men is fully set in them to do evil.

Ecclesiastes 8:11

The Lord is slow to anger and great in power, And will not at all acquit the wicked. The Lord has His way In the whirlwind and in the storm, And the clouds are the dust of His feet.

Nahum 1:3

Then one of the criminals who were hanged blasphemed Him, saying, "If You are the Christ, save Yourself and us." But the other, answering, rebuked him, saying, "Do you not even fear God, seeing you are under the same condemnation? And we indeed justly, for we receive the due reward of our deeds; but this Man has done nothing wrong."
Luke 23:39-41

For the wrath of God is revealed from heaven against all ungodliness and unrighteousness of men, who suppress the truth in unrighteousness,
Romans 1:18

But in accordance with your hardness and your impenitent heart you are treasuring up for yourself wrath in the day of wrath and revelation of the righteous judgment of God, who "will render to each one according to his deeds":

Romans 2:5-6

Therefore whoever resists the authority resists the ordinance of God, and those who resist will bring judgment on themselves.

Romans 13:2

For rulers are not a terror to good works, but to evil. Do you want to be unafraid of the authority? Do what is good, and you will have praise from the same. For he is God's minister to you for good. But if you do evil, be afraid; for he does not bear the sword in vain; for he is God's minister, an avenger to execute wrath on him who practices evil.

Romans 13:3-4

then the Lord knows how to deliver the godly out of temptations and to reserve the unjust under punishment for the day of judgment,

2 Peter 2:9

What The Bible Says About . . .
THE OFFICER'S AUTHORITY

I have taken an oath and confirmed it, that I will follow your righteous laws.
Psalm 119:106 (NIV)

Blessed be the Lord my Rock, Who trains my hands for war, And my fingers for battle—My lovingkindness and my fortress, My high tower and my deliverer, My shield and the One in whom I take refuge, Who subdues my people under me.
Psalm 144:1-2

When the righteous are in authority, the people rejoice; But when a wicked man rules, the people groan.
Proverbs 29:2

Thus says the Lord: "Execute judgment and righteousness, and deliver the plundered out of the hand of the oppressor. Do no wrong and do no violence to the stranger, the fatherless, or the widow, nor shed innocent blood in this place.

Jeremiah 22:3

For I say, through the grace given to me, to everyone who is among you, not to think of himself more highly than he ought to think, but to think soberly, as God has dealt to each one a measure of faith.

Romans 12:3

Likewise the soldiers asked him, saying, "And what shall we do?" So he said to them, "Do not intimidate anyone or accuse falsely, and be content with your wages."

Luke 3:14

Let every soul be subject to the governing authorities. For there is no authority except from God, and the authorities that exist are appointed by God. Therefore whoever resists the authority resists the ordinance of God, and those who resist will bring judgment on themselves. For rulers are not a terror to good works, but to evil. Do you want to be unafraid of the authority? Do what is good, and you will have praise from the same. For he is God's minister to you for good. But if you do evil, be afraid; for he does not bear the sword in vain; for he is God's minister, an avenger to execute wrath on him who practices evil.

Romans 13:1-4

Remind them to be subject to rulers and authorities, to obey, to be ready for every good work,

Titus 3:1

Obey those who rule over you, and be submissive, for they watch out for your souls, as those who must give account. Let them do so with joy and not with grief, for that would be unprofitable for you.

Hebrews 13:17

Therefore submit yourselves to every ordinance of man for the Lord's sake, whether to the king as supreme, or to governors, as to those who are sent by him for the punishment of evildoers and for the praise of those who do good.

1 Peter 2:13-14

What The Bible Says About . . .
BEING ARMED

So Joshua defeated Amalek and his people with the edge of the sword.

Exodus 17:13

Then David put his hand in his bag and took out a stone; and he slung it and struck the Philistine in his forehead, so that the stone sank into his forehead, and he fell on his face to the earth.

1 Samuel 17:49

Then David said to his men, "Every man gird on his sword." So every man girded on his sword, and David also girded on his sword. And about four hundred men went with David, and two hundred stayed with the supplies.

1 Samuel 25:13

And Elisha said to him, "Take a bow and some arrows." So he took himself a bow and some arrows.

2 Kings 13:15

Now these were the numbers of the divisions that were equipped for war, and came to David at Hebron to turn over the kingdom of Saul to him, according to the word of the Lord: of the sons of Judah bearing shield and spear, six thousand eight hundred armed for war;

1 Chronicles 12:23-24

He who scatters has come up before your face. Man the fort! Watch the road! Strengthen your flanks! Fortify your power mightily.

Nahum 2:1

He teaches my hands to make war, So that my arms can bend a bow of bronze. You have also given me the shield of Your salvation; Your right hand has held me up, Your gentleness has made me great. You enlarged my path under me, So my feet did not slip . . . For You have armed me with strength for the battle; You have subdued under me those who rose up against me.

Psalm 18:34-36, 39

Also draw out the spear, And stop those who pursue me. Say to my soul, "I am your salvation."

Psalm 35:3

For I will not trust in my bow, Nor shall my sword save me. But You have saved us from our enemies, And have put to shame those who hated us.

Psalm 44:6-7

Order the buckler and shield, And draw near to battle! Harness the horses, And mount up, you horsemen! Stand forth with your helmets, Polish the spears, Put on the armor!

Jeremiah 46:3-4

For the weapons of our warfare are not carnal but mighty in God for pulling down strongholds,
2 Corinthians 10:4

Put on the whole armor of God, that you may be able to stand against the wiles of the devil. For we do not wrestle against flesh and blood, but against principalities, against powers, against the rulers of the darkness of this age, against spiritual hosts of wickedness in the heavenly places.
Ephesians 6:11-12

For the word of God is living and powerful, and sharper than any two-edged sword, piercing even to the division of soul and spirit, and of joints and marrow, and is a discerner of the thoughts and intents of the heart.

Hebrews 4:12

What The Bible Says About . . .
YOUR CONDUCT AS AN OFFICER

and said to the judges, "Take heed to what you are doing, for you do not judge for man but for the Lord, who is with you in the judgment. Now therefore, let the fear of the Lord be upon you; take care and do it, for there is no iniquity with the Lord our God, no partiality, nor taking of bribes."

2 Chronicles 19:6-7

Blessed is the man Who walks not in the counsel of the ungodly, Nor stands in the path of sinners, Nor sits in the seat of the scornful; But his delight is in the law of the Lord, And in His law he meditates day and night.

Psalm 1:1-2

Do not enter the path of the wicked, And do not walk in the way of evil.

Proverbs 4:14

He who mocks the poor reproaches his Maker; He who is glad at calamity will not go unpunished.

Proverbs 17:5

Do not be envious of evil men, Nor desire to be with them;

Proverbs 24:1

Dead flies putrefy the perfumer's ointment, And cause it to give off a foul odor; So does a little folly to one respected for wisdom and honor.

Ecclesiastes 10:1

For I say, through the grace given to me, to everyone who is among you, not to think of himself more highly than he ought to think, but to think soberly, as God has dealt to each one a measure of faith.

Romans 12:3

Let us walk properly, as in the day, not in revelry and drunkenness, not in lewdness and lust, not in strife and envy.

Romans 13:13

Do not be deceived: "Evil company corrupts good habits."

1 Corinthians 15:33

We give no offense in anything, that our ministry may not be blamed.

2 Corinthians 6:3

Let your gentleness be known to all men. The Lord is at hand.

Philippians 4:5

But you be watchful in all things, endure afflictions, do the work of an evangelist, fulfill your ministry.

2 Timothy 4:5

But no man can tame the tongue. It is an unruly evil, full of deadly poison. With it we bless our God and Father, and with it we curse men, who have been made in the similitude of God. Out of the same mouth proceed blessing and cursing. My brethren, these things ought not to be so.

James 3:8-10

But let none of you suffer as a murderer, a thief, an evildoer, or as a busybody in other people's matters.
1 Peter 4:15

Be sober, be vigilant; because your adversary the devil walks about like a roaring lion, seeking whom he may devour.
1 Peter 5:8

When You Are Called To . . .

When You Are Called To . . .
INTERACT WITH THE PUBLIC

And you shall take no bribe, for a bribe blinds the discerning and perverts the words of the righteous. Also you shall not oppress a stranger, for you know the heart of a stranger, because you were strangers in the land of Egypt.

Exodus 23:8-9

Great peace have those who love Your law, And nothing causes them to stumble.

Psalm 119:165

These six things the Lord hates, Yes, seven are an abomination to Him: A proud look, A lying tongue, Hands that shed innocent blood, A heart that devises wicked plans, Feet that are swift in running to evil, A false witness who speaks lies, And one who sows discord among brethren.

Proverbs 6:16-19

A soft answer turns away wrath, But a harsh word stirs up anger.

Proverbs 15:1

When a man's ways please the Lord, He makes even his enemies to be at peace with him.

Proverbs 16:7

Do not answer a fool according to his folly, Lest you also be like him.

Proverbs 26:4

Learn to do good; Seek justice, Rebuke the oppressor; Defend the fatherless, Plead for the widow.

Isaiah 1:17

bless those who curse you, and pray for those who spitefully use you.

Luke 6:28

Bless those who persecute you; bless and do not curse.

Romans 12:14

Be of the same mind toward one another. Do not set your mind on high things, but associate with the humble. Do not be wise in your own opinion.

Romans 12:16

To the pure all things are pure, but to those who are defiled and unbelieving nothing is pure; but even their mind and conscience are defiled.

Titus 1:15

in all things showing yourself to be a pattern of good works; in doctrine showing integrity, reverence, incorruptibility, sound speech that cannot be condemned, that one who is an opponent may be ashamed, having nothing evil to say of you.

Titus 2:7-8

not returning evil for evil or reviling for reviling, but on the contrary blessing, knowing that you were called to this, that you may inherit a blessing.

1 Peter 3:9

but if you show partiality, you commit sin, and are convicted by the law as transgressors.

James 2:9

When You Are Called To . . .
RESPOND TO DOMESTIC DISTURBANCES

I said, "I will guard my ways, Lest I sin with my tongue; I will restrain my mouth with a muzzle, While the wicked are before me."
Psalm 39:1

Defend the poor and fatherless; Do justice to the afflicted and needy. Deliver the poor and needy; Free them from the hand of the wicked.
Psalm 82:3-4

Hatred stirs up strife, But love covers all sins.
Proverbs 10:12

The merciful man does good for his own soul, But he who is cruel troubles his own flesh.

Proverbs 11:17

A soft answer turns away wrath, But a harsh word stirs up anger.

Proverbs 15:1

Better to dwell in a corner of a housetop, Than in a house shared with a contentious woman.

Proverbs 21:9

The soul of the wicked desires evil; His neighbor finds no favor in his eyes.

Proverbs 21:10

A wicked man hardens his face, But as for the upright, he establishes his way.
> *Proverbs 21:29*

Cast out the scoffer, and contention will leave; Yes, strife and reproach will cease.
> *Proverbs 22:10*

A word fitly spoken is like apples of gold in pictures of silver.
> *Proverbs 25:11*

Do not answer a fool according to his folly, Lest you also be like him.
> *Proverbs 26:4*

Blessed are the peacemakers, For they shall be called sons of God.
> *Matthew 5:9*

Behold, I send you out as sheep in the midst of wolves. Therefore be wise as serpents and harmless as doves.

Matthew 10:16

He will also go before Him in the spirit and power of Elijah, 'to turn the hearts of the fathers to the children,' and the disobedient to the wisdom of the just, to make ready a people prepared for the Lord."

Luke 1:17

Let all bitterness, wrath, anger, clamor, and evil speaking be put away from you, with all malice. And be kind to one another, tenderhearted, forgiving one another, just as God in Christ forgave you.

Ephesians 4:31-32

But if anyone does not provide for his own, and especially for those of his household, he has denied the faith and is worse than an unbeliever.

1 Timothy 5:8

For where envy and self-seeking exist, confusion and every evil thing are there. But the wisdom that is from above is first pure, then peaceable, gentle, willing to yield, full of mercy and good fruits, without partiality and without hypocrisy. Now the fruit of righteousness is sown in peace by those who make peace.

James 3:16-18

Wives, likewise, be submissive to your own husbands, that even if some do not obey the word, they, without a word, may be won by the conduct of their wives . . . Husbands, likewise, dwell with them with understanding, giving honor to the wife, as to the weaker vessel, and as being heirs together of the grace of life, that your prayers may not be hindered.

1 Peter 3:1, 7

When You Are Called To . . .
Deal With Victims, Injury and Death

And when she had opened it, she saw the child, and behold, the baby wept. So she had compassion on him,

Exodus 2:6a

Then the men who were designated by name rose up and took the captives, and from the spoil they clothed all who were naked among them, dressed them and gave them sandals, gave them food and drink, and anointed them; and they let all the feeble ones ride on donkeys. So they brought them to their brethren at Jericho, the city of palm trees. Then they returned to Samaria.

2 Chronicles 28:15

The blessing of a perishing man came upon me, And I caused the widow's heart to sing for joy . . . I was eyes to the blind, And I was feet to the lame . . . Men listened to me and waited, And kept silence for my counsel . . . I chose the way for them, and sat as chief; So I dwelt as a king in the army, As one who comforts mourners.

Job 29:13, 15, 21, 25

The Lord is near to those who have a broken heart, And saves such as have a contrite spirit.

Psalm 34:18

I paced about as though he were my friend or brother; I bowed down heavily, as one who mourns for his mother.

Psalm 35:14

He will redeem their life from oppression and violence; And precious shall be their blood in His sight.

Psalm 72:14

Defend the poor and fatherless; Do justice to the afflicted and needy. Deliver the poor and needy; Free them from the hand of the wicked.

Psalm 82:3-4

Anxiety in the heart of man causes depression, But a good word makes it glad.

Proverbs 12:25

He who mocks the poor reproaches his Maker; He who is glad at calamity will not go unpunished.

Proverbs 17:5

Whoever shuts his ears to the cry of the poor Will also cry himself and not be heard.

Proverbs 21:13

Strengthen the weak hands, And make firm the feeble knees.

Isaiah 35:3

The Lord God has given Me The tongue of the learned, That I should know how to speak A word in season to him who is weary. He awakens Me morning by morning, He awakens My ear To hear as the learned.

Isaiah 50:4

The Spirit of the Lord God is upon Me, Because the Lord has anointed Me To preach good tidings to the poor; He has sent Me to heal the brokenhearted, To proclaim liberty to the captives, And the opening of the prison to those who are bound; To proclaim the acceptable year of the Lord, And the day of vengeance of our God; To comfort all who mourn,

Isaiah 61:1-2

Blessed are the merciful, For they shall obtain mercy.

Matthew 5:7

Even so it is not the will of your Father who is in heaven that one of these little ones should perish.

Matthew 18:14

Give, and it will be given to you: good measure, pressed down, shaken together, and running over will be put into your bosom. For with the same measure that you use, it will be measured back to you.

Luke 6:38

When the Lord saw her, He had compassion on her and said to her, "Do not weep."

Luke 7:13

We then that are strong ought to bear the infirmities of the weak, and not to please ourselves.

Romans 15:1

And now abide faith, hope, love, these three; but the greatest of these is love.

1 Corinthians 13:13

And let us not grow weary while doing good, for in due season we shall reap if we do not lose heart. Therefore, as we have opportunity, let us do good to all, especially to those who are of the household of faith.

Galatians 6:9-10

When You Are Called To . . .
USE INFORMANTS/WORK UNDERCOVER

Take heed to yourself, lest you make a covenant with the inhabitants of the land where you are going, lest it be a snare in your midst.
Exodus 34:12

Rest in the Lord, and wait patiently for Him; Do not fret because of him who prospers in his way, Because of the man who brings wicked schemes to pass.
Psalm 37:7

I said, "I will guard my ways, Lest I sin with my tongue; I will restrain my mouth with a muzzle, While the wicked are before me."
Psalm 39:1

Hear my voice, O God, in my meditation; Preserve my life from fear of the enemy. Hide me from the secret plots of the wicked, From the rebellion of the workers of iniquity,

Psalm 64:1-2

It is better to trust in the Lord Than to put confidence in man.

Psalm 118:8

Direct my steps by Your word, And let no iniquity have dominion over me. Redeem me from the oppression of man, That I may keep Your precepts.

Psalm 119:133-134

Keep me from the snares they have laid for me, And from the traps of the workers of iniquity. Let the wicked fall into their own nets, While I escape safely.

Psalm 141:9-10

Trust in the Lord with all your heart, And lean not on your own understanding; In all your ways acknowledge Him, And He shall direct your paths.

Proverbs 3:5-6

Do not be afraid of sudden terror, Nor of trouble from the wicked when it comes; For the Lord will be your confidence, And will keep your foot from being caught.

Proverbs 3:25-26

A talebearer reveals secrets, But he who is of a faithful spirit conceals a matter.

Proverbs 11:13

The wicked is ensnared by the transgression of his lips, But the righteous will come through trouble.

Proverbs 12:13

A prudent man conceals knowledge, But the heart of fools proclaims foolishness.

Proverbs 12:23

He who guards his mouth preserves his life, But he who opens wide his lips shall have destruction.

Proverbs 13:3

A prudent man foresees evil and hides himself, But the simple pass on and are punished.

Proverbs 22:3

Buy the truth, and do not sell it, Also wisdom and instruction and understanding.

Proverbs 23:23

Confidence in an unfaithful man in time of trouble Is like a bad tooth and a foot out of joint.

Proverbs 25:19

He who hates, disguises it with his lips, And lays up deceit within himself; When he speaks kindly, do not believe him, For there are seven abominations in his heart;

Proverbs 26:24-25

A fool vents all his feelings, But a wise man holds them back.

Proverbs 29:11

Behold, I send you out as sheep in the midst of wolves. Therefore be wise as serpents and harmless as doves.

Matthew 10:16

Watch and pray, lest you enter into temptation. The spirit indeed is willing, but the flesh is weak.

Matthew 26:41

All things are lawful for me, but all things are not helpful. All things are lawful for me, but I will not be brought under the power of any.

1 Corinthians 6:12

When You Are Called To . . .
MAKE AN ARREST

Behold, I send an Angel before you to keep you in the way and to bring you into the place which I have prepared.

Exodus 23:20

No man shall be able to stand against you; the Lord your God will put the dread of you and the fear of you upon all the land where you tread, just as He has said to you.

Deuteronomy 11:25

Be strong and of good courage, do not fear nor be afraid of them; for the Lord your God, He is the One who goes with you. He will not leave you nor forsake you.

Deuteronomy 31:6

The Lord gave them rest all around, according to all that He had sworn to their fathers. And not a man of all their enemies stood against them; the Lord delivered all their enemies into their hand.

Joshua 21:44

Then David said to the Philistine, "You come to me with a sword, with a spear, and with a javelin. But I come to you in the name of the Lord of hosts, the God of the armies of Israel, whom you have defied.

1 Samuel 17:45

So he answered, "Do not fear, for those who are with us are more than those who are with them." And Elisha prayed, and said, "Lord, I pray, open his eyes that he may see." Then the Lord opened the eyes of the young man, and he saw. And behold, the mountain was full of horses and chariots of fire all around Elisha.

2 Kings 6:16-17

For You have armed me with strength for the battle; You have subdued under me those who rose up against me . . . As soon as they hear of me they obey me; The foreigners submit to me.

Psalm 18:39, 44

He delivers me from my enemies. You also lift me up above those who rise against me; You have delivered me from the violent man.

Psalm 18:48

The angel of the Lord encamps all around those who fear Him, And delivers them.

Psalm 34:7

Call upon Me in the day of trouble; I will deliver you, and you shall glorify Me.

Psalm 50:15

You shall not be afraid of the terror by night, Nor of the arrow that flies by day,

Psalm 91:5

For He shall give His angels charge over you, To keep you in all your ways.

Psalm 91:11

O God the Lord, the strength of my salvation, You have covered my head in the day of battle.

Psalm 140:7

Blessed be the Lord my Rock, Who trains my hands for war, And my fingers for battle–My lovingkindness and my fortress, My high tower and my deliverer, My shield and the One in whom I take refuge, Who subdues my people under me.

Psalm 144:1-2

No weapon formed against you shall prosper, And every tongue which rises against you in judgment You shall condemn. This is the heritage of the servants of the Lord, And their righteousness is from Me, Says the Lord.

Isaiah 54:17

Behold, I send you out as sheep in the midst of wolves. Therefore be wise as serpents and harmless as doves.

Matthew 10:16

Bless those who persecute you; bless and do not curse.

Romans 12:14

Put on the whole armor of God, that you may be able to stand against the wiles of the devil. For we do not wrestle against flesh and blood, but against principalities, against powers, against the rulers of the darkness of this age, against spiritual hosts of wickedness in the heavenly places.

Ephesians 6:11-12

I can do all things through Christ who strengthens me.
> *Philippians 4:13*

pray without ceasing,
> *1 Thessalonians 5:17*

not returning evil for evil or reviling for reviling, but on the contrary blessing, knowing that you were called to this, that you may inherit a blessing.
> *1 Peter 3:9*

You are of God, little children, and have overcome them, because He who is in you is greater than he who is in the world.
> *1 John 4:4*

When You Are Called To . . .
CONTROL PRISONERS

I said, "I will guard my ways, Lest I sin with my tongue; I will restrain my mouth with a muzzle, While the wicked are before me."

Psalm 39:1

It is better to trust in the Lord Than to put confidence in man.

Psalm 118:8

Keep me from the snares they have laid for me, And from the traps of the workers of iniquity. Let the wicked fall into their own nets, While I escape safely.

Psalm 141:9-10

He who is slow to anger is better than the mighty, And he who rules his spirit than he who takes a city.

Proverbs 16:32

Do not rob the poor because he is poor, Nor oppress the afflicted at the gate; For the Lord will plead their cause, And plunder the soul of those who plunder them.

Proverbs 22:22-23

Do not rejoice when your enemy falls, And do not let your heart be glad when he stumbles; Lest the Lord see it, and it displease Him, And He turn away His wrath from him.

Proverbs 24:17-18

Do not answer a fool according to his folly, Lest you also be like him.
Proverbs 26:4

Behold, I send you out as sheep in the midst of wolves. Therefore be wise as serpents and harmless as doves.
Matthew 10:16

for I was hungry and you gave Me food; I was thirsty and you gave Me drink; I was a stranger and you took Me in; I was naked and you clothed Me; I was sick and you visited Me; I was in prison and you came to Me . . . And the King will answer and say to them, 'Assuredly, I say to you, inasmuch as you did it to one of the least of these My brethren, you did it to Me.
Matthew 25:35-36, 40

bless those who curse you, and pray for those who spitefully use you.

Luke 6:28

See that no one renders evil for evil to anyone, but always pursue what is good both for yourselves and for all.

1 Thessalonians 5:15

not returning evil for evil or reviling for reviling, but on the contrary blessing, knowing that you were called to this, that you may inherit a blessing.

1 Peter 3:9

but if you show partiality, you commit sin, and are convicted by the law as transgressors.

James 2:9

When You Are Called To . . .
HANDLE EVIDENCE/CONTRABAND

If a person sins and commits a trespass against the Lord by lying to his neighbor about what was delivered to him for safekeeping, or about a pledge, or about a robbery, or if he has extorted from his neighbor, or if he has found what was lost and lies concerning it, and swears falsely—in any one of these things that a man may do in which he sins: then it shall be, because he has sinned and is guilty, that he shall restore what he has stolen, or the thing which he has extorted, or what was delivered to him for safekeeping, or the lost thing which he found,

Leviticus 6:2-4

You shall not steal, nor deal falsely, nor lie to one another.

Leviticus 19:11

You shall do no injustice in judgment, in measurement of length, weight, or volume.

Leviticus 19:35

You shall have a perfect and just weight, a perfect and just measure, that your days may be lengthened in the land which the Lord your God is giving you. For all who do such things, all who behave unrighteously, are an abomination to the Lord your God.

Deuteronomy 25:15-16

Israel has sinned, and they have also transgressed My covenant which I commanded

them. For they have even taken some of the accursed things, and have both stolen and deceived; and they have also put it among their own stuff.
Joshua 7:11

Discretion will preserve you; Understanding will keep you,
Proverbs 2:11

Dishonest scales are an abomination to the Lord, But a just weight is His delight.
Proverbs 11:1

Do not rob the poor because he is poor, Nor oppress the afflicted at the gate; For the Lord will plead their cause, And plunder the soul of those who plunder them.
Proverbs 22:22-23

Behold, My Servant shall deal prudently; He shall be exalted and extolled and be very high.

Isaiah 52:13

He who is faithful in what is least is faithful also in much; and he who is unjust in what is least is unjust also in much.

Luke 16:10

Repay no one evil for evil. Have regard for good things in the sight of all men.

Romans 12:17

Moreover it is required in stewards that one be found faithful.

1 Corinthians 4:2

When You Are Called To . . .
INVESTIGATE

One witness shall not rise against a man concerning any iniquity or any sin that he commits; by the mouth of two or three witnesses the matter shall be established. If a false witness rises against any man to testify against him of wrongdoing, then both men in the controversy shall stand before the Lord, before the priests and the judges who serve in those days.
Deuteronomy 19:15-17

He uncovers deep things out of darkness, And brings the shadow of death to light.
Job 12:22

I was a father to the poor, And I searched out the case that I did not know.

Job 29:16

Indeed I waited for your words, I listened to your reasonings, while you searched out what to say.

Job 32:11

Trust in the Lord with all your heart, And lean not on your own understanding; In all your ways acknowledge Him, And He shall direct your paths.

Proverbs 3:5-6

The simple believes every word, But the prudent considers well his steps.

Proverbs 14:15

Commit your works to the Lord, And your thoughts will be established.

Proverbs 16:3

An evildoer gives heed to false lips; A liar listens eagerly to a spiteful tongue.

Proverbs 17:4

I applied my heart to know, To search and seek out wisdom and the reason of things, To know the wickedness of folly, Even of foolishness and madness.

Ecclesiastes 7:25

Your ears shall hear a word behind you, saying, "This is the way, walk in it," Whenever you turn to the right hand Or whenever you turn to the left.

Isaiah 30:21

Call to Me, and I will answer you, and show you great and mighty things, which you do not know.

Jeremiah 33:3

Behold, I send you out as sheep in the midst of wolves. Therefore be wise as serpents and harmless as doves.

Matthew 10:16

Do not judge according to appearance, but judge with righteous judgment

John 7:24

But the natural man does not receive the things of the Spirit of God, for they are foolishness to him; nor can he know them, because they are spiritually discerned. But he who is spiritual judges all things, yet he himself is rightly judged by no one. For "who has known the mind of the Lord that he may instruct Him?" But we have the mind of Christ.

1 Corinthians 2:14-16

If any of you lacks wisdom, let him ask of God, who gives to all liberally and without reproach, and it will be given to him.

James 1:5

When You Are Called To . . .
WRITE REPORTS

You shall not circulate a false report. Do not put your hand with the wicked to be an unrighteous witness.

Exodus 23:1

If a person sins in hearing the utterance of an oath, and is a witness, whether he has seen or known of the matter–if he does not tell it, he bears guilt.

Leviticus 5:1

I also will answer my part, I too will declare my opinion.

Job 32:17

Every prudent man acts with knowledge,
But a fool lays open his folly.

Proverbs 13:16

Commit your works to the Lord, And your thoughts will be established.

Proverbs 16:3

Do you see a man who excels in his work? He will stand before kings; He will not stand before unknown men.

Proverbs 22:29

The Preacher sought to find acceptable words; and what was written was upright–words of truth.

Ecclesiastes 12:10

"Present your case," says the Lord. "Bring forth your strong reasons," says the King of Jacob.

Isaiah 41:21

I can of Myself do nothing. As I hear, I judge; and My judgment is righteous, because I do not seek My own will but the will of the Father who sent Me.

John 5:30

Do not judge according to appearance, but judge with righteous judgment.

John 7:24

Let all things be done decently and in order.

1 Corinthians 14:40

I can do all things through Christ who strengthens me.

Philippians 4:13

. . . do not become sluggish, but imitate those who through faith and patience inherit the promises.

Hebrews 6:12

If any of you lacks wisdom, let him ask of God, who gives to all liberally and without reproach, and it will be given to him.

James 1:5

When You Are Called To . . .
TESTIFY IN COURT

Now therefore, go, and I will be with your mouth and teach you what you shall say.
Exodus 4:12

You shall not circulate a false report. Do not put your hand with the wicked to be an unrighteous witness.
Exodus 23:1

The mouth of the righteous speaks wisdom, And his tongue talks of justice.
Psalm 37:30

I cling to Your testimonies; O Lord, do not put me to shame!
Psalm 119:31

So shall I have an answer for him who reproaches me, For I trust in Your word.
Psalm 119:42

Set a guard, O Lord, over my mouth; Keep watch over the door of my lips.
Psalm 141:3

Lying lips are an abomination to the Lord, But those who deal truthfully are His delight.
Proverbs 12:22

A true witness delivers souls, But a deceitful witness speaks lies.
Proverbs 14:25

The preparations of the heart belong to man, But the answer of the tongue is from the Lord.
Proverbs 16:1

He who answers a matter before he hears it, It is folly and shame to him.
Proverbs 18:13

Do not answer a fool according to his folly, Lest you also be like him.
Proverbs 26:4

Do you see a man hasty in his words? There is more hope for a fool than for him.
Proverbs 29:20

Do not be rash with your mouth, And let not your heart utter anything hastily before God. For God is in heaven, and you on earth; Therefore let your words be few.

Ecclesiastes 5:2

Do not be afraid of their faces, For I am with you to deliver you," says the Lord. Then the Lord put forth His hand and touched my mouth, and the Lord said to me: "Behold, I have put My words in your mouth.

Jeremiah 1:8-9

for I will give you a mouth and wisdom which all your adversaries will not be able to contradict or resist.

Luke 21:15

Now, Lord, look on their threats, and grant to Your servants that with all boldness they may speak Your word,

Acts 4:29

I can do all things through Christ who strengthens me.

Philippians 4:13

Be diligent to present yourself approved to God, a worker who does not need to be ashamed, rightly dividing the word of truth.

2 Timothy 2:15

For "He who would love life And see good days, Let him refrain his tongue from evil, And his lips from speaking deceit . . ."

1 Peter 3:10

When You Are Called To . . .
CONDUCT AN INTERNAL AFFAIRS INVESTIGATION/ADMINISTER DISCIPLINE

You shall do no injustice in judgment. You shall not be partial to the poor, nor honor the person of the mighty. In righteousness you shall judge your neighbor.

Leviticus 19:15

and said to the judges, "Take heed to what you are doing, for you do not judge for man but for the Lord, who is with you in the judgment. Now therefore, let the fear of the Lord be upon you; take care and do it, for there is no iniquity with the Lord our God, no partiality, nor taking of bribes."

2 Chronicles 19:6-7

For He repays man according to his work,
And makes man to find a reward according to his way.
Job 34:11

Trust in the Lord with all your heart, And lean not on your own understanding;
Proverbs 3:5

Every prudent man acts with knowledge, But a fool lays open his folly.
Proverbs 13:16

Rebuke is more effective for a wise man Than a hundred blows on a fool.
Proverbs 17:10

These things also belong to the wise: It is not good to show partiality in judgment.
Proverbs 24:23

He who rebukes a man will find more favor afterward Than he who flatters with the tongue.

Proverbs 28:23

If a ruler pays attention to lies, All his servants become wicked.

Proverbs 29:12

Also do not take to heart everything people say, Lest you hear your servant cursing you. For many times, also, your own heart has known That even you have cursed others.

Ecclesiastes 7:21-22

For there is no partiality with God.

Romans 2:11

You, therefore, who teach another, do you not teach yourself? You who preach that a man should not steal, do you steal? You who say, "Do not commit adultery," do you commit adultery? You who abhor idols, do you rob temples? You who make your boast in the law, do you dishonor God through breaking the law?

Romans 2:21-23

Repay no one evil for evil. Have regard for good things in the sight of all men.

Romans 12:17

Now I myself am confident concerning you, my brethren, that you also are full of goodness, filled with all knowledge, able also to admonish one another.

Romans 15:14

Do not be deceived, God is not mocked; for whatever a man sows, that he will also reap.
Galatians 6:7

Let all bitterness, wrath, anger, clamor, and evil speaking be put away from you, with all malice. And be kind to one another, tenderhearted, forgiving one another, just as God in Christ forgave you.
Ephesians 4:31-32

If any of you lacks wisdom, let him ask of God, who gives to all liberally and without reproach, and it will be given to him.
James 1:5

but if you show partiality, you commit sin, and are convicted by the law as transgressors.
James 2:9

But the wisdom that is from above is first pure, then peaceable, gentle, willing to yield, full of mercy and good fruits, without partiality and without hypocrisy.

James 3:17

When You Are Called To . . .
DEAL WITH SUPERIORS

If the spirit of the ruler rises against you, Do not leave your post; For conciliation pacifies great offenses.

Ecclesiastes 10:4

The wise in heart will receive commands, But a prating fool will fall.

Proverbs 10:8

The way of a fool is right in his own eyes, But he who heeds counsel is wise.

Proverbs 12:15

Diligent hands will rule, but laziness ends in slave labor.

Proverbs 12:24

Do you see a man who excels in his work? He will stand before kings; He will not stand before unknown men.

Proverbs 22:29

Like the cold of snow in time of harvest Is a faithful messenger to those who send him, For he refreshes the soul of his masters.

Proverbs 25:13

Do not curse the king, even in your thought; Do not curse the rich, even in your bedroom; For a bird of the air may carry your voice, And a bird in flight may tell the matter.

Ecclesiastes 10:20

Most assuredly, I say to you, a servant is not greater than his master; nor is he who is sent greater than he who sent him.
John 13:16

Moreover it is required in stewards that one be found faithful.
1 Corinthians 4:2

nor complain, as some of them also complained, and were destroyed by the destroyer.
1 Corinthians 10:10

Bondservants, be obedient to those who are your masters according to the flesh, with fear and trembling, in sincerity of heart, as to Christ; not with eyeservice, as menpleasers, but as bondservants of Christ, doing the will of God from the heart, with goodwill doing service, as to the Lord, and not to men, knowing that whatever good anyone does, he will receive the same from the Lord, whether he is a slave or free.

Ephesians 6:5-8

Do all things without complaining and disputing,

Philippians 2:14

Bondservants, obey in all things your masters according to the flesh, not with eyeservice, as men-pleasers, but in sincerity of heart, fearing God. And whatever you do, do it heartily, as to the Lord and not to men, knowing that from the Lord you will receive the reward of the inheritance; for you serve the Lord Christ. But he who does wrong will be repaid for what he has done, and there is no partiality.

Colossians 3:22-25

Therefore I exhort first of all that supplications, prayers, intercessions, and giving of thanks be made for all men, for kings and all who are in authority, that we may lead a quiet and peaceable life in all godliness and reverence.

1Timothy 2:1-2

Let as many bondservants as are under the yoke count their own masters worthy of all honor, so that the name of God and His doctrine may not be blasphemed. And those who have believing masters, let them not despise them because they are brethren, but rather serve them because those who are benefited are believers and beloved. Teach and exhort these things.

1Timothy 6:1-2

Exhort bondservants to be obedient to their own masters, to be well pleasing in all things, not answering back, not pilfering, but showing all good fidelity, that they may adorn the doctrine of God our Savior in all things.

Titus 2:9-10

Obey those who rule over you, and be submissive, for they watch out for your souls, as those who must give account. Let them do so with joy and not with grief, for that would be unprofitable for you.

Hebrews 13:17

When You Are Called To . . .
DEAL WITH SUBORDINATES

Now therefore, let the fear of the Lord be upon you; take care and do it, for there is no iniquity with the Lord our God, no partiality, nor taking of bribes.

2 Chronicles 19:7

So look away from him and let him alone, till he has put in his time like a hired man.

Job 14:6

He who rebukes a man will find more favor afterward Than he who flatters with the tongue.

Proverbs 28:23

When the righteous are in authority, the people rejoice; But when a wicked man rules, the people groan.

Proverbs 29:2

If a ruler pays attention to lies, All his servants become wicked.

Proverbs 29:12

Also do not take to heart everything people say, Lest you hear your servant cursing you. For many times, also, your own heart has known That even you have cursed others.

Ecclesiastes 7:21-22

But Jesus called them to Himself and said, "You know that the rulers of the Gentiles lord it over them, and those who are great exercise authority over them. Yet it shall not be so among you; but whoever desires to become great among you, let him be your servant.

Matthew 20:25-26

. . . God, who "will render to each one according to his deeds"

Romans 2:5-6

You, therefore, who teach another, do you not teach yourself? You who preach that a man should not steal, do you steal? You who say, "Do not commit adultery," do you commit adultery? You who abhor idols, do you rob temples? You who make your boast in the law, do you dishonor God through breaking the law?

Romans 2:21-23

And you, masters, do the same things to them, giving up threatening, knowing that your own Master also is in heaven, and there is no partiality with Him.

Ephesians 6:9

Let nothing be done through selfish ambition or conceit, but in lowliness of mind let each esteem others better than himself . . . Let this mind be in you which was also in Christ Jesus, who, being in the form of God, did not consider it robbery to be equal with God, but made Himself of no reputation, taking the form of a bondservant, and coming in the likeness of men.

Philippians 2:3. 5-7

Therefore, as the elect of God, holy and beloved, put on tender mercies, kindness, humility, meekness, longsuffering; bearing with one another, and forgiving one another, if anyone has a complaint against another; even as Christ forgave you, so you also must do. But above all these things put on love, which is the bond of perfection.

Colossians 3:12-14

Masters, give your bondservants what is just and fair, knowing that you also have a Master in heaven.

Colossians 4:1

but if you show partiality, you commit sin, and are convicted by the law as transgressors.

James 2:9

Shepherd the flock of God which is among you, serving as overseers, not by compulsion but willingly, not for dishonest gain but eagerly; nor as being lords over those entrusted to you, but being examples to the flock;

1 Peter 5:2-3

When You Are Called To . . .
SHARE YOUR FAITH

Oh, give thanks to the Lord! Call upon His name; Make known His deeds among the peoples! Sing to Him, sing psalms to Him; Talk of all His wondrous works!
1 Chronicles 16:8-9

Let the redeemed of the Lord say so, Whom He has redeemed from the hand of the enemy,
Psalm 107:2

They shall speak of the glory of Your kingdom, And talk of Your power, To make known to the sons of men His mighty acts, And the glorious majesty of His kingdom.
Psalm 145:11-12

"You are My witnesses," says the Lord, "And My servant whom I have chosen, That you may know and believe Me, And understand that I am He. Before Me there was no God formed, Nor shall there be after Me.
Isaiah 43:10

The Lord has revealed our righteousness. Come and let us declare in Zion the work of the Lord our God.
Jeremiah 51:10

When I say to the wicked, 'O wicked man, you shall surely die!' and you do not speak to warn the wicked from his way, that wicked man shall die in his iniquity; but his blood I will require at your hand. Nevertheless if you warn the wicked to turn from his way, and he does not turn from his way, he shall die in his iniquity; but you have delivered your soul.

Ezekiel 33:8-9

The law of truth was in his mouth, And injustice was not found on his lips. He walked with Me in peace and equity, And turned many away from iniquity.

Malachi 2:6

Let your light so shine before men, that they may see your good works and glorify your Father in heaven.

Matthew 5:16

Also I say to you, whoever confesses Me before men, him the Son of Man also will confess before the angels of God.

Luke 12:8

But you shall receive power when the Holy Spirit has come upon you; and you shall be witnesses to Me in Jerusalem, and in all Judea and Samaria, and to the end of the earth.

Acts 1:8

Walk in wisdom toward those who are outside, redeeming the time. Let your speech always be with grace, seasoned with salt, that you may know how you ought to answer each one.

Colossians 4:5-6

pray without ceasing,

1 Thessalonians 5:17

Therefore do not be ashamed of the testimony of our Lord, nor of me His prisoner,

but share with me in the sufferings for the gospel according to the power of God,
2 Timothy 1:8

saying: "I will declare Your name to My brethren; In the midst of the assembly I will sing praise to You."
Hebrews 2:12

But sanctify the Lord God in your hearts, and always be ready to give a defense to everyone who asks you a reason for the hope that is in you, with meekness and fear; having a good conscience, that when they defame you as evildoers, those who revile your good conduct in Christ may be ashamed. For it is better, if it is the will of God, to suffer for doing good than for doing evil.
1 Peter 3:15-17

When You Are . . .

When You Are . . .
REVILED AND PERSECUTED

The Lord also will be a refuge for the oppressed, A refuge in times of trouble.
Psalm 9:9

For look! The wicked bend their bow, They make ready their arrow on the string, That they may shoot secretly at the upright in heart . . . The Lord tests the righteous, But the wicked and the one who loves violence His soul hates.
Psalm 11:2, 5

Be merciful to me, O God, be merciful to me! For my soul trusts in You; And in the shadow of Your wings I will make my refuge, Until these calamities have passed by.
Psalm 57:1b

Make haste, O God, to deliver me! Make haste to help me, O Lord! Let them be ashamed and confounded Who seek my life; Let them be turned back and confused Who desire my hurt.

Psalm 70:1-2

The proud have forged a lie against me, But I will keep Your precepts with my whole heart . . . Let the proud be ashamed, For they treated me wrongfully with falsehood; But I will meditate on Your precepts . . . All Your commandments are faithful; They persecute me wrongfully; Help me!

Psalm 119:69, 78, 86

Come, my people, enter your chambers, And shut your doors behind you; Hide yourself, as it were, for a little moment, Until the indignation is past.

Isaiah 26:20

For the terrible one is brought to nothing, The scornful one is consumed, And all who watch for iniquity are cut off—

Isaiah 29:20

I, even I, am He who comforts you. Who are you that you should be afraid Of a man who will die, And of the son of a man who will be made like grass?

Isaiah 51:12

No weapon formed against you shall prosper, And every tongue which rises against you in judgment You shall condemn. This is the heritage of the servants of the Lord, And their righteousness is from Me," Says the Lord.

Isaiah 54:17

Blessed are those who are persecuted for righteousness' sake, For theirs is the kingdom of heaven. Blessed are you when they revile and persecute you, and say all kinds of evil against you falsely for My sake.

Matthew 5:10-11

But I say to you, love your enemies, bless those who curse you, do good to those who hate you, and pray for those who spitefully use you and persecute you,

Matthew 5:44

bless those who curse you, and pray for those who spitefully use you.

Luke 6:28

If the world hates you, you know that it hated Me before it hated you.

John 15:18

And not only that, but we also glory in tribulations, knowing that tribulation produces perseverance; and perseverance, character; and character, hope. Now hope does not disappoint, because the love of God has been poured out in our hearts by the Holy Spirit who was given to us.

Romans 5:3-5

Bless those who persecute you; bless and do not curse.

Romans 12:14

Repay no one evil for evil. Have regard for good things in the sight of all men. If it is possible, as much as depends on you, live peaceably with all men. Beloved, do not avenge yourselves, but rather give place to wrath; for it is written, "Vengeance is Mine, I will repay," says the Lord. Therefore "If your enemy is hungry, feed him; If he is thirsty, give him a drink; For in so doing you will heap coals of fire on his head." Do not be overcome by evil, but overcome evil with good.

Romans 12:17-21

And we labor, working with our own hands. Being reviled, we bless; being persecuted, we endure;
1 Corinthians 4:12

But in all things we commend ourselves as ministers of God: in much patience, in tribulations, in needs, in distresses,
2 Corinthians 6:4

pray without ceasing,
1 Thessalonians 5:17

For consider Him who endured such hostility from sinners against Himself, lest you become weary and discouraged in your souls.

Hebrews 12:3

Therefore it is also contained in the Scripture, "Behold, I lay in Zion A chief cornerstone, elect, precious, And he who believes on Him will by no means be put to shame."

1 Peter 2:6

For this is the will of God, that by doing good you may put to silence the ignorance of foolish men—

1 Peter 2:15

Beloved, do not think it strange concerning the fiery trial which is to try you, as though some strange thing happened to you; but rejoice to the extent that you partake of Christ's sufferings, that when His glory is revealed, you may also be glad with exceeding joy.

1 Peter 4:12-13

Do not marvel, my brethren, if the world hates you.

1 John 3:13

When You Are . . .
ANGRY

Do not hasten in your spirit to be angry,
For anger rests in the bosom of fools.

Ecclesiastes 7:9

Cease from anger, and forsake wrath; Do not fret–it only causes harm.

Psalm 37:8

A wise man fears and departs from evil, But a fool rages and is self-confident . . . He who is slow to wrath has great understanding, But he who is impulsive exalts folly.

Proverbs 14:16, 29

A soft answer turns away wrath, But a harsh word stirs up anger.

Proverbs 15:1

He who is slow to anger is better than the mighty, And he who rules his spirit than he who takes a city.

Proverbs 16:32

An angry man stirs up strife, And a furious man abounds in transgression.

Proverbs 29:22

Then the Lord said, "Is it right for you to be angry?"

Jonah 4:4

But I say to you that whoever is angry with his brother without a cause shall be in danger of the judgment. And whoever says to his brother, 'Raca!' shall be in danger of the council. But whoever says,

'You fool!' shall be in danger of hell fire. Therefore if you bring your gift to the altar, and there remember that your brother has something against you, leave your gift there before the altar, and go your way. First be reconciled to your brother, and then come and offer your gift.

Matthew 5:22-24

For if you forgive men their trespasses, your heavenly Father will also forgive you. But if you do not forgive men their trespasses, neither will your Father forgive your trespasses.

Matthew 6:14-15

Beloved, do not avenge yourselves, but rather give place to wrath; for it is written, "Vengeance is Mine, I will repay," says the Lord.

Romans 12:19

"Be angry, and do not sin": do not let the sun go down on your wrath, nor give place to the devil . . . Let all bitterness, wrath, anger, clamor, and evil speaking be put away from you, with all malice. And be kind to one another, tenderhearted, forgiving one another, just as God in Christ forgave you.

Ephesians 4:26-27, 31-32

But now you yourselves are to put off all these: anger, wrath, malice, blasphemy, filthy language out of your mouth.

Colossians 3:8

So then, my beloved brethren, let every man be swift to hear, slow to speak, slow to wrath; for the wrath of man does not produce the righteousness of God.

James 1:19-20

When You Are . . .
DISCOURAGED

You will show me the path of life; In Your presence is fullness of joy; At Your right hand are pleasures forevermore.
Psalm 16:11

Wait on the Lord; Be of good courage, And He shall strengthen your heart; Wait, I say, on the Lord!
Psalm 27:14

Serve the Lord with gladness; Come before His presence with singing.
Psalm 100:2

Though I walk in the midst of trouble, You will revive me; You will stretch out Your hand Against the wrath of my enemies, And Your right hand will save me.

Psalm 138:7

My son, do not despise the chastening of the Lord, Nor detest His correction; For whom the Lord loves He corrects, Just as a father the son in whom he delights.

Proverbs 3:11-12

Commit your works to the Lord, And your thoughts will be established.

Proverbs 16:3

For a righteous man may fall seven times And rise again, But the wicked shall fall by calamity.

Proverbs 24:16

So the ransomed of the Lord shall return, And come to Zion with singing, With everlasting joy on their heads. They shall obtain joy and gladness; Sorrow and sighing shall flee away.

Isaiah 51:11

But Jesus looked at them and said, "With men it is impossible, but not with God; for with God all things are possible."

Mark 10:27

Let not your heart be troubled; you believe in God, believe also in Me.

John 14:1

For in it the righteousness of God is revealed from faith to faith; as it is written, "The just shall live by faith."

Romans 1:17

He did not waver at the promise of God through unbelief, but was strengthened in faith, giving glory to God, and being fully convinced that what He had promised He was also able to perform.

Romans 4:20-21

Now may the God of hope fill you with all joy and peace in believing, that you may abound in hope by the power of the Holy Spirit.

Romans 15:13

Now thanks be to God who always leads us in triumph in Christ, and through us diffuses the fragrance of His knowledge in every place.
2 Corinthians 2:14

And let us not grow weary while doing good, for in due season we shall reap if we do not lose heart.
Galatians 6:9

being confident of this very thing, that He who has begun a good work in you will complete it until the day of Jesus Christ;
Philippians 1:6

And my God shall supply all your need according to His riches in glory by Christ Jesus.
Philippians 4:19

Rejoice always, pray without ceasing, in everything give thanks; for this is the will of God in Christ Jesus for you.

1 Thessalonians 5:16-18

You therefore, my son, be strong in the grace that is in Christ Jesus . . . You therefore must endure hardship as a good soldier of Jesus Christ.

2 Timothy 2:1, 3

Therefore do not cast away your confidence, which has great reward.

Hebrews 10:35

In this you greatly rejoice, though now for a little while, if need be, you have been grieved by various trials, that the genuineness of your faith, being much more precious than gold that perishes, though it is tested by fire, may be found to praise, honor, and glory at the revelation of Jesus Christ,

1 Peter 1:6-7

Beloved, do not think it strange concerning the fiery trial which is to try you, as though some strange thing happened to you; but rejoice to the extent that you partake of Christ's sufferings, that when His glory is revealed, you may also be glad with exceeding joy.

1 Peter 4:12-13

When You Are . . .
UNDER STRESS

And He said, "My Presence will go with you, and I will give you rest."

Exodus 33:14

Now acquaint yourself with Him, and be at peace; Thereby good will come to you.

Job 22:21

The Lord will give strength to His people; The Lord will bless His people with peace.

Psalm 29:11

Call upon Me in the day of trouble; I will deliver you, and you shall glorify Me.

Psalm 50:15

Cast your burden on the Lord, And He shall sustain you; He shall never permit the righteous to be moved.

Psalm 55:22

My flesh and my heart fail; But God is the strength of my heart and my portion forever.

Psalm 73:26

In the day of my trouble I will call upon You, For You will answer me.

Psalm 86:7

Return to your rest, O my soul, For the Lord has dealt bountifully with you.

Psalm 116:7

When you lie down, you will not be afraid; Yes, you will lie down and your sleep will be sweet.

Proverbs 3:24

You will keep him in perfect peace, Whose mind is stayed on You, Because he trusts in You.

Isaiah 26:3

Come to Me, all you who labor and are heavy laden, and I will give you rest. Take My yoke upon you and learn from Me, for I am gentle and lowly in heart, and you will find rest for your souls.

Matthew 11:28-29

And He said to them, "Come aside by yourselves to a deserted place and rest a while." For there were many coming and going, and they did not even have time to eat.

Mark 6:31

So He Himself often withdrew into the wilderness and prayed.

Luke 5:16

Peace I leave with you, My peace I give to you; not as the world gives do I give to you. Let not your heart be troubled, neither let it be afraid.

John 14:27

For to be carnally minded is death, but to be spiritually minded is life and peace.

Romans 8:6

Rejoice in the Lord always. Again I will say, rejoice! Let your gentleness be known to all men. The Lord is at hand. Be anxious for nothing, but in everything by prayer and supplication, with thanksgiving, let your requests be made known to God; and the peace of God, which surpasses all understanding, will guard your hearts and minds through Christ Jesus.

Philippians 4:4-7

And let the peace of God rule in your hearts, to which also you were called in one body; and be thankful.

Colossians 3:15

Pray without ceasing,

1 Thessalonians 5:17

There remains therefore a rest for the people of God. For he who has entered His rest has himself also ceased from his works as God did from His. Let us therefore be diligent to enter that rest, lest anyone fall according to the same example of disobedience.

Hebrews 4:9-11

Let us therefore come boldly to the throne of grace, that we may obtain mercy and find grace to help in time of need.

Hebrews 4:16

When You Are . . .
BURNED OUT

But He knows the way that I take; When He has tested me, I shall come forth as gold.
Job 23:10

My flesh and my heart fail; But God is the strength of my heart and my portion forever.
Psalm 73:26

And not only that, but we also glory in tribulations, knowing that tribulation produces perseverance; and perseverance, character; and character, hope. Now hope does not disappoint, because the love of God has been poured out in our hearts by the Holy Spirit who was given to us.
Romans 5:3-5

And do not be conformed to this world, but be transformed by the renewing of your mind, that you may prove what is that good and acceptable and perfect will of God.

Romans 12:2

For we do not wrestle against flesh and blood, but against principalities, against powers, against the rulers of the darkness of this age, against spiritual hosts of wickedness in the heavenly places.

Ephesians 6:12

Brethren, I do not count myself to have apprehended; but one thing I do, forgetting those things which are behind and reaching forward to those things which are ahead, I press toward the goal for the prize of the upward call of God in Christ Jesus.

Philippians 3:13-14

Rejoice in the Lord always. Again I will say, rejoice!

Philippians 4:4

And my God shall supply all your need according to His riches in glory by Christ Jesus.

Philippians 4:19

strengthened with all might, according to His glorious power, for all patience and longsuffering with joy; giving thanks to the Father who has qualified us to be partakers of the inheritance of the saints in the light.

Colossians 1:11-12

For this reason I also suffer these things; nevertheless I am not ashamed, for I know whom I have believed and am persuaded that He is able to keep what I have committed to Him until that Day.
2 Timothy 1:12

Therefore we also, since we are surrounded by so great a cloud of witnesses, let us lay aside every weight, and the sin which so easily ensnares us, and let us run with endurance the race that is set before us,
Hebrews 12:1

Therefore strengthen the hands which hang down, and the feeble knees, and make straight paths for your feet, so that what is lame may not be dislocated, but rather be healed. Pursue peace with all people, and holiness, without which no one will see the Lord: looking carefully lest anyone fall short of the grace of God; lest any root of bitterness springing up cause trouble, and by this many become defiled;

Hebrews 12:12-15

For whatever is born of God overcomes the world. And this is the victory that has overcome the world–our faith. Who is he who overcomes the world, but he who believes that Jesus is the Son of God?

1 John 5:4-5

Beloved, I pray that you may prosper in all things and be in health, just as your soul prospers.

3 John 1:2

And he who overcomes, and keeps My works until the end, to him I will give power over the nations—

Revelation 2:26

When You Are . . .
HARDENED/EMBITTERED

Do not harden your hearts, as in the rebellion, As in the day of trial in the wilderness,

Psalm 95:8

Search me, O God, and know my heart; Try me, and know my anxieties; And see if there is any wicked way in me, And lead me in the way everlasting.

Psalm 139:23-24

Let not mercy and truth forsake you; Bind them around your neck, Write them on the tablet of your heart, And so find favor and high esteem In the sight of God and man.

Proverbs 3:3-4

Keep your heart with all diligence, For out of it spring the issues of life.
Proverbs 4:23

Happy is the man who is always reverent, But he who hardens his heart will fall into calamity.
Proverbs 28:14

Thus says the Lord: "For three transgressions of Edom, and for four, I will not turn away its punishment, Because he pursued his brother with the sword, And cast off all pity; His anger tore perpetually, And he kept his wrath forever.
Amos 1:11

O Lord, I have heard your speech and was afraid; O Lord, revive Your work in the midst of the years! In the midst of the years make it known; In wrath remember mercy.

Habakkuk 3:2

bless those who curse you, and pray for those who spitefully use you.

Luke 6:28

You have neither part nor portion in this matter, for your heart is not right in the sight of God. Repent therefore of this your wickedness, and pray God if perhaps the thought of your heart may be forgiven you. For I see that you are poisoned by bitterness and bound by iniquity.

Acts 8:21-23

But in accordance with your hardness and your impenitent heart you are treasuring up for yourself wrath in the day of wrath and revelation of the righteous judgment of God, who "will render to each one according to his deeds": eternal life to those who by patient continuance in doing good seek for glory, honor, and immortality; but to those who are self-seeking and do not obey the truth, but obey unrighteousness–indignation and wrath, tribulation and anguish, on every soul of man who does evil, of the Jew first and also of the Greek;
Romans 2:5-9

Let all bitterness, wrath, anger, clamor, and evil speaking be put away from you, with all malice.

Ephesians 4:31

Brethren, I do not count myself to have apprehended; but one thing I do, forgetting those things which are behind and reaching forward to those things which are ahead, I press toward the goal for the prize of the upward call of God in Christ Jesus. Therefore let us, as many as are mature, have this mind; and if in anything you think otherwise, God will reveal even this to you.

Philippians 3:13-15

but exhort one another daily, while it is called "Today," lest any of you be hardened through the deceitfulness of sin. For we have become partakers of Christ if we hold the beginning of our confidence steadfast to the end, while it is said: "Today, if you will hear His voice,

Do not harden your hearts as in the rebellion."
Hebrews 3:13-15

Pursue peace with all people, and holiness, without which no one will see the Lord: looking carefully lest anyone fall short of the grace of God; lest any root of bitterness springing up cause trouble, and by this many become defiled;
Hebrews 12:14-15

When You Are . . .
IMPRESSED WITH YOUR OWN AUTHORITY

I will break the pride of your power; I will make your heavens like iron and your earth like bronze.

Leviticus 26:19

Talk no more so very proudly; Let no arrogance come from your mouth, For the Lord is the God of knowledge; And by Him actions are weighed.

1 Samuel 2:3

The wicked in his proud countenance does not seek God; God is in none of his thoughts . . . He has said in his heart, "I shall not be moved; I shall never be in adversity." His mouth is full of cursing and deceit and oppression; Under his tongue is trouble and iniquity.

Psalm 10:4, 6-7

Whoever secretly slanders his neighbor, Him I will destroy; The one who has a haughty look and a proud heart, Him I will not endure.

Psalm 101:5

Lord, my heart is not haughty, Nor my eyes lofty. Neither do I concern myself with great matters, Nor with things too profound for me.

Psalm 131:1

Surely He scorns the scornful, But gives grace to the humble.

Proverbs 3:34

The fear of the Lord is to hate evil; Pride and arrogance and the evil way And the perverse mouth I hate.

Proverbs 8:13

The fear of the Lord is the instruction of wisdom, And before honor is humility.

Proverbs 15:33

Pride goes before destruction, And a haughty spirit before a fall.

Proverbs 16:18

A haughty look, a proud heart, And the plowing of the wicked are sin.

Proverbs 21:4

It is not good to eat much honey; So to seek one's own glory is not glory.
Proverbs 25:27

A man's pride will bring him low, But the humble in spirit will retain honor.
Proverbs 29:23

Woe to those who are wise in their own eyes, And prudent in their own sight!
Isaiah 5:21

Therefore whoever humbles himself as this little child is the greatest in the kingdom of heaven.
Matthew 18:4

Yet it shall not be so among you; but whoever desires to become great among you, let him be your servant.
Matthew 20:26

And He sat down, called the twelve, and said to them, "If anyone desires to be first, he shall be last of all and servant of all."
Mark 9:35

For whoever exalts himself will be humbled, and he who humbles himself will be exalted.
Luke 14:11

For I say, through the grace given unto me, to every man that is among you, not to think of himself more highly than he ought to think ; but to think soberly, according as God hath dealt to every man the measure of faith.

Romans 12:3 (KJV)

casting down arguments and every high thing that exalts itself against the knowledge of God, bringing every thought into captivity to the obedience of Christ,;

2 Corinthians 10:5

Let us not become conceited, provoking one another, envying one another.

Galatians 5:26

For if anyone thinks himself to be something, when he is nothing, he deceives himself.

Galatians 6:3

When You Are . . .
THE SUBJECT OF AN INTERNAL AFFAIRS INVESTIGATION

Nevertheless the Lord your God would not listen to Balaam, but the Lord your God turned the curse into a blessing for you, because the Lord your God loves you.
Deuteronomy 23:5

For His anger is but for a moment, His favor is for life; Weeping may endure for a night, But joy comes in the morning.
Psalm 30:5

Be merciful to me, O God, be merciful to me! For my soul trusts in You; And in the shadow of Your wings I will make my refuge, Until these calamities have passed by.
Psalm 57:1

I am weary with my crying; My throat is dry; My eyes fail while I wait for my God. Those who hate me without a cause Are more than the hairs of my head; They are mighty who would destroy me, Being my enemies wrongfully; Though I have stolen nothing, I still must restore it. O God, You know my foolishness; And my sins are not hidden from You . . . But as for me, my prayer is to You, O Lord, in the acceptable time; O God, in the multitude of Your mercy, Hear me in the truth of Your salvation. Deliver me out of the mire, And let me not sink; Let me be delivered from those who hate me, And out of the deep waters.

Psalm 69:3-5, 13-14

My soul melts from heaviness; Strengthen me according to Your word.

Psalm 119:28

Search me, O God, and know my heart; Try me, and know my anxieties; And see if there is any wicked way in me, And lead me in the way everlasting.

Psalm 139:23-24

Trust in the Lord with all your heart, And lean not on your own understanding;

Proverbs 3:5

My son, do not despise the chastening of the Lord, Nor detest His correction; For whom the Lord loves He corrects, Just as a father the son in whom he delights.

Proverbs 3:11-12

Poverty and shame will come to him who disdains correction, But he who regards a rebuke will be honored.

Proverbs 13:18

When a man's ways please the Lord, He makes even his enemies to be at peace with him.

Proverbs 16:7

He who covers his sins will not prosper, But whoever confesses and forsakes them will have mercy.

Proverbs 28:13

For the Lord God will help Me; Therefore I will not be disgraced; Therefore I have set My face like a flint, And I know that I will not be ashamed.

Isaiah 50:7

And we know that all things work together for good to those who love God, to those who are the called according to His purpose.

Romans 8:28

No temptation has overtaken you except such as is common to man; but God is faithful, who will not allow you to be tempted beyond what you are able, but with the temptation will also make the way of escape, that you may be able to bear it.
1 Corinthians 10:13

Be anxious for nothing, but in everything by prayer and supplication, with thanksgiving, let your requests be made known to God; and the peace of God, which surpasses all understanding, will guard your hearts and minds through Christ Jesus.
Philippians 4:6-7

Let your speech always be with grace, seasoned with salt, that you may know how you ought to answer each one.
Colossians 4:6

Blessed is the man who endures temptation; for when he has been approved, he will receive the crown of life which the Lord has promised to those who love Him. Let no one say when he is tempted, "I am tempted by God"; for God cannot be tempted by evil, nor does He Himself tempt anyone.

James 1:12-13

Indeed we count them blessed who endure. You have heard of the perseverance of Job and seen the end intended by the Lord–that the Lord is very compassionate and merciful.

James 5:11

For what credit is it if, when you are beaten for your faults, you take it patiently? But when you do good and suffer, if you take it patiently, this is commendable before God.

1 Peter 2:20

For the eyes of the Lord are on the righteous, And His ears are open to their prayers; But the face of the Lord is against those who do evil." And who is he who will harm you if you become followers of what is good? But even if you should suffer for righteousness' sake, you are blessed. "And do not be afraid of their threats, nor be troubled." But sanctify the Lord God in your hearts, and always be ready to give a defense to everyone who asks you a reason for the hope that is in you, with meekness and fear; having a good conscience, that when they defame you as evildoers, those who revile your good conduct in

Christ may be ashamed. For it is better, if it is the will of God, to suffer for doing good than for doing evil.

1 Peter 3:12-17

casting all your care upon Him, for He cares for you.

1 Peter 5:7

When You Need . . .

When You Need . . .
PROTECTION

Only do not rebel against the Lord, nor fear the people of the land, for they are our bread; their protection has departed from them, and the Lord is with us. Do not fear them.
Numbers 14:9

The Lord will cause your enemies who rise against you to be defeated before your face; they shall come out against you one way and flee before you seven ways.
Deuteronomy 28:7

No man shall be able to stand before you all the days of your life; as I was with Moses, so I will be with you. I will not leave you nor forsake you.

Joshua 1:5

Stay with me; do not fear. For he who seeks my life seeks your life, but with me you shall be safe.

1 Samuel 22:23

And you would be secure, because there is hope; Yes, you would dig around you, and take your rest in safety.

Job 11:18

The angel of the Lord encamps all around those who fear Him, And delivers them.

Psalm 34:7

Be merciful to me, O God, be merciful to me! For my soul trusts in You; And in the shadow of Your wings I will make my refuge, Until these calamities have passed by.

Psalm 57:1

He who dwells in the secret place of the Most High Shall abide under the shadow of the Almighty. I will say of the Lord, "He is my refuge and my fortress; My God, in Him I will trust." Surely He shall deliver you from the snare of the fowler And from the perilous pestilence. He shall cover you with His feathers, And under His wings you shall take refuge; His truth shall be your shield and buckler.

Psalm 91:1-4

A thousand may fall at your side, And ten thousand at your right hand; But it shall not come near you.

Psalm 91:7

My help comes from the Lord, Who made heaven and earth. He will not allow your foot to be moved; He who keeps you will not slumber. Behold, He who keeps Israel Shall neither slumber nor sleep . . . The Lord shall preserve you from all evil; He shall preserve your soul. The Lord shall preserve your going out and your coming in From this time forth, and even forevermore.

Psalm 121:2-4, 7-8

But whoever listens to me will dwell safely, And will be secure, without fear of evil.

Proverbs 1:33

So shall they fear The name of the Lord from the west, And His glory from the rising of the sun; When the enemy comes in like a flood, The Spirit of the Lord will lift up a standard against him.

Isaiah 59:19

But there shall not an hair of your head perish.
Luke 21:18

by the word of truth, by the power of God, by the armor of righteousness on the right hand and on the left,
2 Corinthians 6:7

But the Lord is faithful, who will establish you and guard you from the evil one.
2 Thessalonians 3:3

Let us therefore come boldly to the throne of grace, that we may obtain mercy and find grace to help in time of need.
Hebrews 4:16

When You Need . . .
COURAGE

After these things the word of the Lord came to Abram in a vision, saying, "Do not be afraid, Abram. I am your shield, your exceedingly great reward."

Genesis 15:1

No man shall be able to stand before you all the days of your life; as I was with Moses, so I will be with you. I will not leave you nor forsake you . . . Have I not commanded you? Be strong and of good courage; do not be afraid, nor be dismayed, for the Lord your God is with you wherever you go.

Joshua 1:5, 9

The Lord is my light and my salvation; Whom shall I fear? The Lord is the strength of my life; Of whom shall I be afraid? When the wicked came against me To eat up my flesh, My enemies and foes, They stumbled and fell. Though an army may encamp against me, My heart shall not fear; Though war should rise against me, In this I will be confident.

Psalm 27:1-3

Wait on the Lord; Be of good courage, And He shall strengthen your heart; Wait, I say, on the Lord!

Psalm 27:14

I sought the Lord, and He heard me, And delivered me from all my fears.

Psalm 34:4

He shall cover you with His feathers, And under His wings you shall take refuge; His truth shall be your shield and buckler. You shall not be afraid of the terror by night, Nor of the arrow that flies by day, Nor of the pestilence that walks in darkness, Nor of the destruction that lays waste at noonday. A thousand may fall at your side, And ten thousand at your right hand; But it shall not come near you.

Psalm 91:4-7

The Lord is on my side; I will not fear. What can man do to me?

Psalm 118:6

But whoever listens to me will dwell safely, And will be secure, without fear of evil.

Proverbs 1:33

Do not be afraid of sudden terror, Nor of trouble from the wicked when it comes; For the Lord will be your confidence, And will keep your foot from being caught.

Proverbs 3:25-26

Fear not, for I am with you; Be not dismayed, for I am your God. I will strengthen you, Yes, I will help you, I will uphold you with My righteous right hand.

Isaiah 41:10

In righteousness you shall be established; You shall be far from oppression, for you shall not fear; And from terror, for it shall not come near you.

Isaiah 54:14

Peace I leave with you, my peace I give unto you: not as the world gives, give I unto you. Let not your heart be troubled, neither let it be afraid.

John 14:27

For you did not receive the spirit of bondage again to fear, but you received the Spirit of adoption by whom we cry out, "Abba, Father." . . . What then shall we say to these things? If God is for us, who can be against us?

Romans 8:15, 31

I can do all things through Christ who strengthens me.

Philippians 4:13

Pray without ceasing.

1 Thessalonians 5:17

For God has not given us a spirit of fear, but of power and of love and of a sound mind.

2 Timothy 1:7

So we may boldly say: "The Lord is my helper; I will not fear. What can man do to me?"

Hebrews 13:6

When You Need . . .
STRENGTH

The Lord is my strength and song, And He has become my salvation; He is my God, and I will praise Him; My father's God, and I will exalt Him.
Exodus 15:2

And now, I pray, let the power of my Lord be great, just as You have spoken . . .
Numbers 14:17a

God is my strength and power, And He makes my way perfect.
2 Samuel 22:33

Seek the Lord and His strength; Seek His face evermore!
1 Chronicles 16:11

Both riches and honor come from You, And You reign over all. In Your hand is power and might; In Your hand it is to make great And to give strength to all.

1 Chronicles 29:12

Be ye strong therefore, and let not your hands be weak: for your work shall be rewarded. But you, be strong and do not let your hands be weak, for your work shall be rewarded!

2 Chronicles 15:7

God is our refuge and strength, A very present help in trouble.

Psalm 46:1b

Sing aloud to God our strength; Make a joyful shout to the God of Jacob.

Psalm 81:1b

He gives power to the weak, And to those who have no might He increases strength..
Isaiah 40:29

Fear not, for I am with you; Be not dismayed, for I am your God. I will strengthen you, Yes, I will help you, I will uphold you with My righteous right hand.
Isaiah 41:10

Watch and pray, lest you enter into temptation. The spirit indeed is willing, but the flesh is weak.
Mark 14:38

For the kingdom of God is not in word but in power.
1 Corinthians 4:20

Not that we have dominion over your faith, but are fellow workers for your joy; for by faith you stand.
2 Corinthians 1:24

And He said to me, "My grace is sufficient for you, for My strength is made perfect in weakness." Therefore most gladly I will rather boast in my infirmities, that the power of Christ may rest upon me.
2 Corinthians 12:9

And I thank Christ Jesus our Lord who has enabled me, because He counted me faithful, putting me into the ministry,
1Timothy 1:12

For God has not given us a spirit of fear, but of power and of love and of a sound mind.
2 Timothy 1:7

You are of God, little children, and have overcome them, because He who is in you is greater than he who is in the world.
1 John 4:4

When You Need . . .
WISDOM

And to man He said, 'Behold, the fear of the Lord, that is wisdom, And to depart from evil is understanding.'

Job 28:28

The fear of the Lord is the beginning of wisdom; A good understanding have all those who do His commandments. His praise endures forever.

Psalm 111:10

He stores up sound wisdom for the upright; He is a shield to those who walk uprightly; He guards the paths of justice, And preserves the way of His saints. Then

you will understand righteousness and justice, Equity and every good path.
Proverbs 2:7-9

In all your ways acknowledge Him, And He shall direct your paths.
Proverbs 3:6

A wise man fears and departs from evil, But a fool rages and is self-confident.
Proverbs 14:16

The words of a wise man's mouth are gracious, But the lips of a fool shall swallow him up;
Ecclesiastes 10:12

Therefore whoever hears these sayings of Mine, and does them, I will liken him to a wise man who built his house on the rock: and the rain descended, the floods came, and the winds blew and beat on that house; and it did not fall, for it was founded on the rock.

Matthew 7:24-25

for I will give you a mouth and wisdom which all your adversaries will not be able to contradict or resist.

Luke 21:15

But of Him you are in Christ Jesus, who became for us wisdom from God–and righteousness and sanctification and redemption—

1 Corinthians 1:30

However, we speak wisdom among those who are mature, yet not the wisdom of this age, nor of the rulers of this age, who are coming to nothing. But we speak the wisdom of God in a mystery, the hidden wisdom which God ordained before the ages for our glory . . . But God has revealed them to us through His Spirit. For the Spirit searches all things, yes, the deep things of God. For what man knows the things of a man except the spirit of the man which is in him? Even so no one knows the things of God except the Spirit of God. Now we have received, not the spirit of the world, but the Spirit who is from God, that we might know the things that have been freely given to us by God.

1 Corinthians 2:6-7, 10-12

Let no one deceive himself. If anyone among you seems to be wise in this age, let him become a fool that he may become wise.
1 Corinthians 3:18

Beware lest anyone cheat you through philosophy and empty deceit, according to the tradition of men, according to the basic principles of the world, and not according to Christ.
Colossians 2:8

All Scripture is given by inspiration of God, and is profitable for doctrine, for reproof, for correction, for instruction in righteousness, that the man of God may be complete, thoroughly equipped for every good work.
2 Timothy 3:16-17

If any of you lacks wisdom, let him ask of God, who gives to all liberally and without reproach, and it will be given to him.

James 1:5

Who is wise and understanding among you? Let him show by good conduct that his works are done in the meekness of wisdom . . . But the wisdom that is from above is first pure, then peaceable, gentle, willing to yield, full of mercy and good fruits, without partiality and without hypocrisy.

James 3:13, 17

When You Need . . .
SELF-CONTROL

But some rebels said, "How can this man save us?" So they despised him, and brought him no presents. But he held his peace.
1 Samuel 10:27

Let the Lord judge between you and me, and let the Lord avenge me on you. But my hand shall not be against you.
1 Samuel 24:12

Keep your tongue from evil, And your lips from speaking deceit.
Psalm 34:13

I said, "I will guard my ways, Lest I sin with my tongue; I will restrain my mouth with a muzzle, While the wicked are before me."

Psalm 39:1

He who guards his mouth preserves his life, But he who opens wide his lips shall have destruction.

Proverbs 13:3

He who is slow to anger is better than the mighty, And he who rules his spirit than he who takes a city.

Proverbs 16:32

Whoever has no rule over his own spirit Is like a city broken down, without walls.

Proverbs 25:28

Therefore do not let sin reign in your mortal body, that you should obey it in its lusts.

Romans 6:12

But I discipline my body and bring it into subjection, lest, when I have preached to others, I myself should become disqualified.

1 Corinthians 9:27

But the fruit of the Spirit is love, joy, peace, longsuffering, kindness, goodness, faithfulness,

Galatians 5:22

Set your mind on things above, not on things on the earth.

Colossians 3:2

If anyone among you thinks he is religious, and does not bridle his tongue but deceives his own heart, this one's religion is useless.

James 1:26

For we all stumble in many things. If anyone does not stumble in word, he is a perfect man, able also to bridle the whole body.

James 3:2

For "He who would love life And see good days, Let him refrain his tongue from evil, And his lips from speaking deceit. Let him turn away from evil and do good; Let him seek peace and pursue it. For the eyes of the Lord are on the righteous, And His ears are open to their prayers;

But the face of the Lord is against those who do evil."

1 Peter 3:10-12

But also for this very reason, giving all diligence, add to your faith virtue, to virtue knowledge, to knowledge self-control, to self-control perseverance, to perseverance godliness,

2 Peter 1:5-6

When You Need . . .
FAITH

Have I not commanded you? Be strong and of good courage; do not be afraid, nor be dismayed, for the Lord your God is with you wherever you go.

Joshua 1:9

How precious is Your lovingkindness, O God! Therefore the children of men put their trust under the shadow of Your wings.

Psalm 36:7

O Israel, trust in the Lord; He is their help and their shield.

Psalm 115:9

I will go before you And make the crooked places straight; I will break in pieces the gates of bronze And cut the bars of iron.
Isaiah 45:2

So Jesus said to them, "Because of your unbelief; for assuredly, I say to you, if you have faith as a mustard seed, you will say to this mountain, 'Move from here to there,' and it will move; and nothing will be impossible for you.
Matthew 17:20

And when He had come into the house, the blind men came to Him. And Jesus said to them, "Do you believe that I am able to do this?" They said to Him, "Yes, Lord." Then He touched their eyes, saying, "According to your faith let it be to you."

Matthew 9:28-29

Jesus said to him, "If you can believe, all things are possible to him who believes."

Mark 9:23

For with God nothing will be impossible.

Luke 1:37

Let not your heart be troubled; you believe in God, believe also in Me . . . Most assuredly, I say to you, he who believes in Me, the works that I do he will do also; and greater works than these he will do, because I go to My Father. And whatever you ask in My name, that I will do, that

the Father may be glorified in the Son. If you ask anything in My name, I will do it.
John 14:1, 12-14

For in it the righteousness of God is revealed from faith to faith; as it is written, "The just shall live by faith."
Romans 1:17

For I say, through the grace given to me, to everyone who is among you, not to think of himself more highly than he ought to think, but to think soberly, as God has dealt to each one a measure of faith.
Romans 12:3

So then faith comes by hearing, and hearing by the word of God.
Romans 10:17

For we walk by faith, not by sight.
> *2 Corinthians 5:7*

Now faith is the substance of things hoped for, the evidence of things not seen.
> *Hebrews 11:1*

But without faith it is impossible to please Him, for he who comes to God must believe that He is, and that He is a rewarder of those who diligently seek Him.
> *Hebrews 11:6*

looking unto Jesus, the author and finisher of our faith, who for the joy that was set before Him endured the cross, despising the shame, and has sat down at the right hand of the throne of God.
> *Hebrews 12:2*

that the genuineness of your faith, being much more precious than gold that perishes, though it is tested by fire, may be found to praise, honor, and glory at the revelation of Jesus Christ, whom having not seen you love. Though now you do not see Him, yet believing, you rejoice with joy inexpressible and full of glory,

1 Peter 1:7-8

For whatever is born of God overcomes the world. And this is the victory that has overcome the world–our faith.

1 John 5:4

When You Need . . .
FORGIVENESS

I will cleanse them from all their iniquity by which they have sinned against Me, and I will pardon all their iniquities by which they have sinned and by which they have transgressed against Me.

Jeremiah 33:8

Blessed is he whose transgression is forgiven, Whose sin is covered. Blessed is the man to whom the Lord does not impute iniquity, And in whose spirit there is no deceit.

Psalm 32:1-2

You have forgiven the iniquity of Your people; You have covered all their sin. Selah

Psalm 85:2

For You, Lord, are good, and ready to forgive, And abundant in mercy to all those who call upon You.

Psalm 86:5

As far as the east is from the west, So far has He removed our transgressions from us.

Psalm 103:12

"Come now, and let us reason together," Says the Lord, "Though your sins are like scarlet, They shall be as white as snow; Though they are red like crimson, They shall be as wool.

Isaiah 1:18

I, even I, am He who blots out your transgressions for My own sake; And I will not remember your sins.

Isaiah 43:25

Let the wicked forsake his way, And the unrighteous man his thoughts; Let him return to the Lord, And He will have mercy on him; And to our God, For He will abundantly pardon.

Isaiah 55:7

Therefore if you bring your gift to the altar, and there remember that your brother has something against you, leave your gift there before the altar, and go your way. First be reconciled to your brother, and then come and offer your gift.

Matthew 5:23-24

And whenever you stand praying, if you have anything against anyone, forgive him, that your Father in heaven may also forgive you your trespasses.
Mark 11:25

Judge not, and you shall not be judged. Condemn not, and you shall not be condemned. Forgive, and you will be forgiven.
Luke 6:37

Blessed are those whose lawless deeds are forgiven, And whose sins are covered;
Romans 4:7

bearing with one another, and forgiving one another, if anyone has a complaint against another; even as Christ forgave you, so you also must do.

Colossians 3:13

If we confess our sins, He is faithful and just to forgive us our sins and to cleanse us from all unrighteousness.

1 John 1:9

For if our heart condemns us, God is greater than our heart, and knows all things.

1 John 3:20

When You Need . . .
JOY

Then he said to them, "Go your way, eat the fat, drink the sweet, and send portions to those for whom nothing is prepared; for this day is holy to our Lord. Do not sorrow, for the joy of the Lord is your strength."
Nehemiah 8:10

I will be glad and rejoice in You; I will sing praise to Your name, O Most High. When my enemies turn back, They shall fall and perish at Your presence.
Psalm 9:2-3

You will show me the path of life; In Your presence is fullness of joy; At Your right hand are pleasures forevermore.
Psalm 16:11

For His anger is but for a moment, His favor is for life; Weeping may endure for a night, But joy comes in the morning.

Psalm 30:5

I will bless the Lord at all times; His praise shall continually be in my mouth.

Psalm 34:1

Restore to me the joy of Your salvation, And uphold me by Your generous Spirit.

Psalm 51:12

Will You not revive us again, That Your people may rejoice in You?

Psalm 85:6

The Lord has done great things for us, And we are glad . . . Those who sow in tears Shall reap in joy. He who continually goes forth weeping, Bearing seed for sowing, Shall doubtless come again with rejoicing, Bringing his sheaves with him.

Psalm 126:3, 5-6

He who heeds the word wisely will find good,
And whoever trusts in the Lord, happy is he.

Proverbs 16:20

Until now you have asked nothing in My name. Ask, and you will receive, that your joy may be full.

John 16:24

Great is my boldness of speech toward you, great is my boasting on your behalf. I am filled with comfort. I am exceedingly joyful in all our tribulation.

2 Corinthians 7:4

Therefore I take pleasure in infirmities, in reproaches, in needs, in persecutions, in distresses, for Christ's sake. For when I am weak, then I am strong.

2 Corinthians 12:10

strengthened with all might, according to His glorious power, for all patience and longsuffering with joy; giving thanks to the Father who has qualified us to be partakers of the inheritance of the saints in the light.

Colossians 1:11-12

My brethren, count it all joy when you fall into various trials, knowing that the testing of your faith produces patience.

James 1:2-3

but rejoice to the extent that you partake of Christ's sufferings, that when His glory is revealed, you may also be glad with exceeding joy.

1 Peter 4:13

Notes

Notes

Notes

Notes

Notes

Notes

Notes

Notes

Made in the USA
Columbia, SC
20 February 2023